If Knowing God Is So Great, Why Am I Afraid?

Sally Greiner Roach

LIGUORI
PUBLICATIONS

One Liguori Drive
Liguori, Missouri 63057-9999
(314) 464-2500

Dedication

*To Tom, my husband, who is my support and
friend through all of life's challenges.
S.G.R.*

Imprimi Potest:
William A. Nugent, C.SS.R.
Provincial, St. Louis Province
The Redemptorists

Imprimatur:
Monsignor Maurice F. Byrne
Vice Chancellor, Archdiocese of St. Louis

ISBN 0-89243-318-3
Library of Congress Catalog Card Number: 89-063856

Copyright © 1990, Liguori Publications
Printed in U.S.A.

Scripture texts used in this work are taken from THE NEW AMERICAN
BIBLE WITH REVISED NEW TESTAMENT, copyright © 1986, by the
Confraternity of Christian Doctrine, Washington, DC 20017, and
are used by permission of copyright owner. All rights reserved.

TABLE OF CONTENTS

Prologue 5

1. If Knowing God Is So Great, Why Am I Afraid? 9
An Explorative Process 13
Fear of Asking 16

2. Why Do People Keep Pushing the Bible at Me? 21
An Enormous Leap 24

3. How Can I Talk With Someone I Can't See or Hear? . . . 35
God Speaks Through Formal Prayer 36
God Speaks Through Daily Events 38
God Speaks Through Forgiveness 41
God Speaks by Using Us as His Instruments 46
God Speaks Through Suffering 50
God Speaks Through Nature 53
God Speaks Through Art, Music, and Dance 55
God Speaks to Each of Us 57

4. Can God Possibly Love Someone Like Me? 58
God Wants to Guide Us 65

5. Is This Stuff Really From God? 69

    Use Everyday Communication Skills 70

    Notice Feelings, Thoughts, and Changes 71

    Is It Good? 73

    Is It to My Advantage? 74

    Does It Stand the Test of Time? 75

    Does Enthusiasm Develop? 76

    Does a Sense of Urgency Develop? 77

    Do I Feel at Peace? 78

    Ask for Signs 80

    Ask Another Christian to Pray 83

    Do I Seem to Be Controlling God? 84

    How Can I Be Sure When God Speaks? 85

6. Surely God Wouldn't Call Someone Like Me? 87

    We Are Called in Big Ways and Small 92

    My First Call Is to Pray 95

About the Author 96

PROLOGUE

God active in my life? No way! I was a confirmed skeptic. Now I believe that God speaks with me daily. I believe it is helpful to be aware of God's counsel in order to make full use of it, but the communication is not contingent on belief. I want to share my growing realization that God communicates with all of us regularly. You may wonder why I say this so confidently. You might think I'm a religious fanatic or that I am particularly blessed by God. (I am particularly blessed, but no more than you.) Some may speculate that I am well-intentioned but mistaken.

It seems strange to be writing a book. I am not a writer, nor has being a writer ever been my fantasy. My urge to write began recently as my sister was preparing for a pilgrimage to Medjugorje, Yugoslavia. It is the custom for friends and family to send written petitions for pilgrims to present there. I wrote petitions, but also asked her to bring me a message concerning my future professional plans. She replied, "I'll try, but I don't feel I'm capable of receiving messages — I'll try." I was stunned. Only then did I realize the magnitude of the change in me over these last eight years. My reply to her letter made me want to write this book. In it I share with you how scared I was when I first encountered God. I discuss various methods of prayer, as well as ways to decide when God is speaking.

I have changed from a woman who only occasionally referred

to God in crisis situations or when my Catholic cultural heritage pushed me toward important rites of passage like Baptism and First Communion to one who communicates with God regularly. I now live my life with the knowledge of that communication as my base. I feel whole, comfortable, and at peace in a way I never have before. That's not to say I don't struggle sometimes or get discouraged. Sometimes I try to convince myself that I must be hearing the wrong counsel — or the right counsel. God calls me to do the wildest things. Living is now an adventure.

I hope to continue growing in intimacy with God. When I am able to love with a pure heart, I will have no need for prayer methods or formulas for getting in touch with God. I will have no need for the love taps of answered prayer. I will never wonder when God is speaking. I will be able to let go of my own ego and all the world's distractions and be free to live in constant awareness of God's presence. In the meantime I must find my way owning my limitations and gifts. Please know that this is my journey only. I make no claim that this is the "right" way or that it is even particularly commonplace. This is my beginning. I present, for your use in any small way, my faltering and inadequate steps toward knowing God.

This part of my journey began eight years ago when our daughter, who was ten years old at the time, came home from school asking, "Which Church do we go to?"

"Catholic," I replied. "Don't you remember making your First Communion two years ago?"

"Oh, yeah, I guess so," she replied as she left to play with the little neighbor girl.

I take my role as mother and watchdog for the home very seriously. My job is to notice all the small things happening to the children and eventually to discuss necessary developments with my husband to keep him abreast of activities in the home. After my daughter's question I began musing on the role of the Church in my childhood, in my marriage, and in the lives of others. I hated to

6

think about one of our three daughters getting married in a church she had never attended. What if one of their husbands died and she had no place to have the funeral? It seemed wrong to leave a child ill-prepared for big events like marriage and death. The more I reflected, the more this seemed like something we, as parents, needed to discuss.

I was a free-thinking, well-traveled, intelligent adult who made her own decisions based on logic and common sense. I liked a social life full of parties, drinking, and talk about politics and international issues. I read the newspaper faithfully, as well as Stephen King, James Michener, and a few added romance novels. I readily admitted to being bogged down by the role the world placed on me as a woman. I fought against placing family above professional satisfaction for a few years but eventually embraced the role of mother and wife, at least while the children were young. The pull on my mind and heart of the effort to balance family and profession was an ongoing problem.

Spiritual balance? I wouldn't have known what that was. I didn't pray, go to church, or talk about spiritual topics. I saw those who did as narrow and dull individuals. I assumed that they were naive at best, unless they were priests or pastors, who were, after all, paid as professionals to do that sort of thing. The world needs a few, I thought.

Though logic told me that I didn't belong at church now, I was glad I could go with confidence to my local Catholic Church when I needed it. I began to think we should leave at least that security to our children. Attend church, yes. Get involved, no. So we decided at least to try attending church.

Logic got me into the church. Once I was there, God had to use extreme measures to get a hardheaded person like me to pay attention. Initially I attributed the experiences to imagination and emotional fatigue. I tried denial and avoidance. I didn't want to get involved. I didn't want to be taken for a fool. I argued with myself,

7

with logic, and with my basic view of the world. God is persistent and patient. This experience of God, and the transformation of my world-view and system of living, is the subject of this book. I am still logical, free thinking, and intelligent. I still value my marriage and children. I still see the church as a place to be married and buried and as a crutch in times of need. I still struggle with my role as a woman in today's world, my role as mother and professional. I still read Stephen King and James Michener occasionally and the newspaper regularly. But God, who loves me just as I am, has joined my life. He has joined my logical thinking mind, my marriage, my Church, my thought processes and decision-making. My attitude toward life is now one of awareness of God in everything. I have put away the romance novel for Scripture and spiritual reading. I still love a party and tipping a couple of bourbons, but the conversation includes where people stand with God and how God affects their lives. I still use all the logic and thought processes available to me, along with standing before God and waiting for counsel. So I am the same, but different — very different.

I wish to acknowledge the many people who helped me to complete this book. I am especially grateful to my friend Terry Marshall, who I tell everyone is the "real writer" that spent hours putting little red marks on the original manuscript so that I could then work to make it presentable to Liguori. He taught me to write. Other family and friends contributed their stories and suggestions: Dorothy Germain, Don Greiner, Ken and Leitner Greiner, Lynn Hopkins, Billie Greiner Kannady, Father Xavier Manovath, Elayne Mayrides, Kathy Mundie, Edna Nequette, Maurie Ockerman, Connie Greiner Robb, Peggy Ronan, Eithna Sullivan and, of course, Tom and my children Susheela, Shanti, and Sherifa.

Sally Greiner Roach
Fairfax, Virginia
March 1989

CHAPTER 1

IF KNOWING GOD
IS SO GREAT,
WHY AM I AFRAID?

I felt anxiety at my first encounter with God, although it seems I should have felt pleased and excited. Initially I didn't understand the total implications of the encounter. But logic told me I should at least be happy, perhaps gathering friends around me to sing and dance and praise God with joy. Some people do respond this way. But many people are fearful, nervous, anxious, or agitated when they are healed, observe a miracle, or are otherwise touched by God for the first time. Most are simply overwhelmed.

When I was the unsuspecting recipient of God's "zapping," I was afraid — afraid of the unknown. Suddenly I saw the power of God and my own helplessness, and this was fearsome because I valued control in my life and normally avoided situations I couldn't control. No religious fanatic, I had little patience with overactive imaginations. A loving God who communicates with ordinary human beings like me was something I had dismissed as extreme. No, I was not a glad participant that first time.

Fear is a common response to an encounter with God. The Bible is filled with examples. For instance, when the woman who had been afflicted with hemorrhages for twelve years realized she had been healed, she "approached [Jesus] in fear and trembling. She fell down before Jesus and told him the whole truth. He said to her, 'Daughter, your faith has saved you. Go in peace and be cured of your affliction' " (Mark 5:33-34).

Again in Luke we learn:

Now there were shepherds in that region living in the fields and keeping the night watch over their flock. The angel of the Lord appeared to them and the glory of the Lord shone around them, and they were struck with great fear. The angel said to them, "Do not be afraid; for behold, I proclaim to you good news of great joy that will be for all the people."

(Luke 2:8-10)

Even Mary, known for her great faith, was fearful at first when the angel announced the birth of Jesus. The angel reassured her with these words: "Do not be afraid, Mary, for you have found favor with God" (Luke 1:30).

Knowing that others were also afraid at their first encounter with God is comforting to me. My conversion story clearly shows that early fear. Our daughters were ten, seven, and five when we decided to go to church again. Dressed up in high heels and nylons on a Sunday morning, I stood next to three squirming kids in the midst of about eight hundred people. Considering that the Sunday newspaper was at home on the dining-room table and a pot of coffee brewed, this was not my first choice for a pleasant Sunday morning.

Then suddenly some words in the middle of a hymn stunned me with new meaning, and I felt as though I were the only person in the crowded church. I shook all over, tears streaming down my face. Then, inexplicably, I knew that my husband, Tom, and I were going to lead marriage retreats in another country. This knowledge was so far-fetched I wondered if I was hallucinating. We would never give personal talks in public! I was shaken to the core. No, I didn't have a vision which allowed me to see into the future. No, I didn't hear a voice. No, I can't describe more clearly what it was like to "just know" the future. Nor can I explain why I cried on and on without reason. None of this fit into my logical world. To say I was upset is putting it mildly. On the way out of church I worried about what to tell Tom, who stood beside me wondering why I had filled up his handkerchief. I was determined to put these ideas out of my mind and just hoped I wouldn't have to answer any questions.

All the next week, no matter what I was doing, the experience nagged at me. I tried to escape, to rationalize my strange behavior, by concluding that it was the power of suggestion. Tom and I had recently been on a marriage retreat, and I had been touched by the generosity and openness of the presenting couples on that weekend. I was amazed that they were willing to share so intimately with us. It was a wonderful weekend, but *I* wasn't going to talk about my personal life in public! I didn't think Tom would either, and at that time we weren't even thinking about going overseas. It all seemed a little strange, but as the week progressed I began to feel confident I had just experienced a new aspect of my own imagination. It was over. I wasn't going to worry about it, and I certainly wasn't going to lead retreats!

Sunday came again. Again the worshipers around me receded, and I stood alone. This marriage thing again! No visions. No voice. Just knowing. Comprehending. It was as if a major network had selected me to be televised in childbirth or to describe on a talk show the loss of my job or the state of my finances.

The fireworks came not in the transfer of knowledge but in my reaction. I was crying again. By this time my family thought I had gone off my rocker. For that matter, I too thought maybe I was ready for the couch.

Through another week I worried. I am a well-controlled individual, not prone to emotional outbursts. Yet something extraordinary had happened, and I could no longer ignore or dismiss my behavior. Could this possibly be real? Was I having a mental breakdown? Did I need professional help? I certainly couldn't tell anyone, for surely my story would be met with laughter. As another Sunday approached, I was afraid to go to church. I was curious, but I was afraid — afraid I wouldn't be able to ignore what was happening to me; afraid I would have to reveal myself; afraid this might be real; afraid it might not be real. I began to suspect that this was an experience with God. After all, it did happen in church. If God was talking to me, then I was afraid of the repercussions this would have on my life, on our lives as a married couple; afraid I might really have to stand in front of people and tell them about my personal life; afraid I would make a fool of myself. If it wasn't real, then I was sick.

Things got worse before they got better. The third Sunday I suddenly felt certain the priest saying Mass was in trouble. Although he looked healthy, I knew that he was physically ill, and worse, that he was feeling deserted by God. He needed to know that God was with him. I should go to him, I thought. Again I shook all over, and tears rolled down my face. I was confused and scared. When Mass was over, I again became aware of the crowd bustling around me. I wiped my face, blew my nose, smiled at Tom in embarrassment, and walked with determination out of the church.

This had gone too far. We had just started attending church again regularly, and I didn't know any of the parish priests — not even their names! Imagine a priest's response to this kind of overture! If the idea of leading marriage retreats seemed ridiculous, this approached the absurd. As the week passed, I tried to push away the thought of next Sunday. I didn't want to walk into that church. I considered not going, but that would cause a scene at home. Why not simply announce that I didn't want to go to church because God was giving me messages that I didn't want to hear? No way. God didn't communicate with people directly — or did he? In any event I knew Tom wouldn't believe it.

With dread I made my way to the church the following Sunday. When I saw that another priest was saying Mass, I felt a little better. All went well through the homily, and I relaxed a little, thinking, "Whew! This horrible dream is finally over!"

Then came the petitions. "For rapid healing of our pastor, who was admitted to the hospital this week, we pray to the Lord."

"Lord, hear our prayer," the congregation responded.

I almost collapsed. My mind shouted, "No! I should have contacted him. I knew this was coming. This is my fault." The rest of the liturgy passed in a blur. I felt guilty and in turmoil, but my doubts about the reality of these encounters were gone. There was a real person in the hospital, and I had known he was sick before he did. I didn't doubt now that he was also in a spiritual desert. He needed help.

When we got home, I put our oldest daughter in charge and took Tom to the bedroom. I closed the door, burst into tears, and incoherently told him the whole story. He just listened, then said, "You should visit Father in the hospital, and for your own peace of mind, you need to find out if this sort of thing happens to other people."

An Explorative Process

When I called the rectory to find out which hospital the pastor was in only to be told he couldn't have visitors, I felt as if a huge load had been lifted from my shoulders. After all, I had tried to contact the priest. That should satisfy God! I pictured myself standing beside his hospital bed. Of course, he is dressed in black and wearing a Roman collar! I float a few feet off the ground and straighten my halo as I say, "Father, don't worry. God loves you. He told me so." I might even give him my blessing. This could be funny. But not today!

That week I went to the church office and made an appointment with another priest. I tried to be businesslike during this meeting, but some background was necessary before my questions even made sense. Soon I choked up, hardly able to speak. "Does God speak to ordinary, unsaintly doubters?" I asked. "Could what is happening to me be from God?" Wanting some kind of confirmation, I also asked if the sick pastor was in spiritual trauma. The priest told me that God does occasionally speak, but he couldn't say whether my experience was with God. And he wouldn't say anything about the sick pastor.

When I have a problem, I gather information, assess it, then act. And I had a problem! After all that had happened, I had to do something; I couldn't just ignore the experience. I didn't know exactly what I was supposed to do, but as an information gatherer I wanted facts and opinions, not spooky stories about the experience of God. I also didn't want to have Church doctrine quoted to me.

I was too intimidated to approach active Christians for advice because they seemed so confident in their beliefs about God. Besides, in my confusion and embarrassment I didn't even know what type of questions to ask, and I was fearful and hesitant about relating my own experience. Why did I keep quiet? I needed to be able to ask questions in a "proper" setting without appearing foolish. Even now I find it hard to share my experiences of God; then, I felt positively weird. If I had begun talking about "God's plan" and the listener had laughed or found it to be an "interesting concept," I would have been embarrassed.

As I became bolder, however, I began to ask questions of believers and attend workshops. Another way I was able to gather information without having to speak out was by reading. I must have read at least a hundred books with various testimonies about

God's way. I read about miracles. I read about famous healers. I wish now that I had taken notes, but I didn't have time for that. I inhaled information as fast as I could find it.

This series of events began an exploration process that has not ceased to this day. I believe now that God speaks to all of us, and not just occasionally. I believe that he does it every day because he loves us.

Eight years ago I walked through life assuming that since God created this beautiful world, he would help me out in times of need. I would fulfill my duty by baptizing my children and even trying to go to church most Sundays. I was conditioned to be suspicious of religious fanaticism. Then God came into my life, and the experience he brought me told me something like this: "I'm part of your life every day, Sally. I'll help you and guide you. I know that you are hardheaded and not likely to believe me; so to prove it I will give you knowledge of the future." I was afraid and confused, so I began to explore God's actions in my life. I began to trust experience — mine and others'.

Several years later we moved overseas and were asked to lead marriage weekends. This awakening changed my expectations of myself and others and of what is important in my life. My attitudes and behavior patterns needed drastic adjustments. Up until that time I had operated my life without referring to God, so my immediate response was to be overwhelmed and fearful. I didn't understand yet that God helps and makes possible all of the changes each step of the way. God's whole "package" takes time to absorb. It transformed my life right down to the way I do daily activities. It called me to become dependent on God. No wonder I felt scared.

Only recently I found out by coincidence that our pastor, the one I thought I should visit in the hospital, had indeed gone through a spiritual crisis and transformation. By the time I heard this news, it only confirmed what I had already come to know and accept.

Now I believe that God operates actively in my life and wants to help me. He answers my questions and advises me. So why am I sometimes still afraid to ask him questions? Let's address that question, the fear of asking, in the next section.

Fear of Asking

Even confirmed believers sometimes hesitate to ask God for guidance. Turn first to Scripture to understand this phenomenon. Jesus and the apostles must have been a friendly group. Jesus was certainly the spiritual leader, the teacher; yet there were other strong personalities in the group. We know, for example, that Judas held the money. The apostles were Jesus' advance men. They organized the meals and other daily needs and must have laughed and joked together often. Jesus was a sought-after dinner guest. Stuffy? No way. Even the Pharisees vied with one another to get him to visit their homes, risking the intrusion of prostitutes and tax collectors. Yet, despite his openness, adaptability, charm, and wit, even his own disciples were afraid to question him.

> They did not understand this saying; its meaning was hidden from them so that they should not understand it, and they were afraid to ask him about this saying.
>
> (Luke 9:45)

Why was it that even Jesus' disciples were afraid to ask him about the matter? Scripture doesn't give explanations, but human nature and our own reactions may give some insights. We are told to "ask and it will be given to you" and "to the one who knocks, the door will be opened" (Matthew 7:7,8). So I know that God wants me to ask, yet I hesitate. I am fearful of asking any more questions. This fear isn't a terrified fear. I know that Jesus isn't going to strike me dead. The apostles knew it too. Instead it is an anxiety, a nervousness.

There are a number of possible reasons for anxiety when dealing with Jesus. He is unpredictable. He often puts us on the spot. He asks us to do things before we think we are ready. He wants us to do the hard things. He knows our weaknesses and challenges us in just that part of our lives we don't want to face. Sometimes he doesn't seem to answer our prayers. He asks us to release control of our lives. Yes, a relationship with Jesus can cause anxiety.

Recently I realized with surprise that I still sometimes avoid asking God for help. I was having an attack of "fear of asking" about my professional plans. Afterward I realized that I didn't want to ask for fear of his answer! I didn't want to reevaluate the established priorities in my life — priorities I spent years developing. First comes my relationship with God, then my marriage, then my children, and finally professional satisfaction.

When I left my childhood home, I was sure good mothering was my most important life goal. I soon realized, however, that mothering wasn't going to be my highest life priority. For a few years professional success became my priority and, I assumed, my ticket to happiness. But eventually I decided that it too was wrong for me. Then I focused on my marriage. More recently I've come to understand these various priorities as distinct but related. Each takes effort, but they must be put in perspective or life gets out of balance. Figuring all this out has caused stress and pressure over the years, but I pride myself on my flexibility and willingness to evaluate even tough personal issues. I want to do God's will, yet I was seven years into my newfound belief that God loves, counsels, and guides me and didn't want to consult God because I thought he might ask too much. I thought he might mess with my priorities.

Setting my priorities doesn't mean that in any given day's activities I must spend my time, money, energy, and heart in any particular order. Sometimes the job looms large and has many pressures; sometimes a child is in trouble; and sometimes the sticky floor needs more attention than our marriage. By priorities I mean the direction and purpose my life should take. Deciding what to do with my life, even with definite priorities established, can get very complicated. I didn't want God confusing me with his guidance.

When my sister wrote that she wanted to pray with me, I realized how anxious I was about asking God for guidance. I had been puzzling and stewing for months. I had done my homework, and now it was time to let go and let God have input into my decision-making process. It was appropriate that I should write a book. My first priority, my relationship with God, would certainly be in focus, since the book would be about communication with God. My second and third priorities, my marriage and children, would be more in my control since I would be working at home. My fourth priority, professional challenge, would certainly be fulfilled beyond my wildest expectation if I actually produced a book.

God can be creative with his suggestions. But I had never in my whole life even considered writing a book; so I was scared. I didn't know if I had the necessary skills. I dreaded the pained looks of family and friends when I said, "I'm writing a book about communication with God!" Some succeeded at keeping their faces blank. One said sarcastically, "And how long do you think this will take — four years?" Another said, "Come on, Sally, this is nuts, a waste of time. Why don't you apply for a real job?" I was hurt but still determined. It can be scary to ask questions of God.

I had been fearful and upset at my first encounter with God, but even as a more mature Christian I found myself afraid to ask God for guidance. This phenomenon appears in Scripture, but is this fear commonplace for today's Christians? When I asked friends to share experiences of fear or anxiety in their relationship with God, one answered, "I have not experienced the 'fear phenomenon' you addressed...." Another friend wrote, "Some of the points don't seem to relate to my experiences, for example, 'fear of asking.' I never had that. I've not had much of the negative aspects like anxiety or a troubled spirit."

But it wasn't just me who experienced the "fear phenomenon." Another friend wrote, "I have also experienced the 'fear of asking.' I grew up thinking that I shouldn't bother God with my minuscule problems when he had such great things on his mind. On the one hand, I didn't expect him to be interested. On the other, I think I feared he might be angry that I bothered him and consider me unappreciative of all he had given me already. I feared calling attention to myself. After all, I knew I really could be a better person. Maybe he would point that out too. Maybe it was a trade-off, and I didn't deserve his special favors."

It seemed with the passage of years that as a Christian I shouldn't feel tension and fear anymore. Having experienced the "peace of God that surpasses all understanding" (Philippians 4:7), I should never again fear responding to God or asking for guidance. Since I had been making decisions with God for years and had never been given a bum steer, why the hesitation? Sometimes God challenges long-held beliefs or attitudes as he did when he tapped me in church. Sometimes his challenge is to action, as it was in writing this book. Always it is difficult, and often it is scary.

The apostles, who were with him day in day out for three years, felt fear and lacked faith while trying to follow Jesus. They cowered in the upper room in fear after Jesus' death. Peter, in fear, denied Jesus vehemently three times shortly after he was arrested (see Luke 22:54-62). The story of Peter walking on the water illustrates fear and resistance in the experienced Christian:

Peter said to him in reply, "Lord, if it is you, command me to come to you on the water." He said, "Come." Peter got out of the boat and began to walk on the water toward Jesus. But when he saw how [strong] the wind was he became frightened; and, beginning to sink, he cried out, "Lord, save me!" Immediately Jesus stretched out his hand and caught him, and said to him, "O you of little faith, why did you doubt?" After they got into the boat, the wind died down.

(Matthew 14:28-32)

Another important message in this story is that Peter did get out of the boat. Like Peter, we are called to get out of our boats even when we are afraid. Peter was with Jesus every day, and still he was frightened. But he called out for help when he began to sink. Fear must be motivating, not debilitating. A friend tells how she makes fear and uncertainty productive. "If I try to anticipate or figure out what God wants me to do next, confusion can easily set in. What I have learned to do is step out in my uncertainty and pray that I will understand if I have made the right move."

Because my initial encounter with God came as such a surprise and because I was ignorant and reluctant, I was fearful. This fear changed as I became more confident, manifesting itself as a fear of asking. I didn't recognize it at first. It came disguised. I wasn't ready to accept that I could be afraid of God, because I had finally learned to know God as a friend.

Since fear and anxiety when dealing with God are not unusual, we should search for their cause rather than deny their existence. It is important to recognize that fear is not necessarily a negative sign in our relationship with God but often the signal for a call to growth. We can be confident that God is going to challenge us more than we would ever challenge ourselves. If we accept the challenge God places before us, then we must make some kind of change. Change can be scary, but it stimulates growth. Fear, if used as a motivating factor, allows us to be bold, because though we are afraid we know we are fully supported by God in everything we do.

CHAPTER 2

WHY DO PEOPLE KEEP PUSHING THE BIBLE AT ME?

The Bible serves as a resource for knowledge about what God is like. It can help keep us on track as we struggle to communicate better. Do you want to know about the origins of Christianity? Check the Bible. Do you want to know how Jesus behaved? Check the Bible. Do you want to know how to pray? Check the Bible. Do you want comfort or direction? Check the Bible. Until recently I thought the Bible was a code of ethics with a few stories thrown in to make it more readable. It was also useful at funerals and weddings. I had no idea I would eventually use the Bible as a guide for my life and a resource to develop intimacy with God. Even after I was touched by God, I still didn't want to read the Bible. In fact, I became angry when people suggested that I should.

I grew up with little formal training in the Bible, learning only enough Scripture quotes to answer questions frequently asked of Catholics. Catholics were not highly regarded in Oklahoma where

I was raised, and as a child my faith was challenged often. I needed to know how to answer, so I memorized the biblical bases for such Catholic beliefs as papal infallibility: "You are Peter, and upon this rock I will build my church, and the gates of the netherworld shall not prevail against it" (Matthew 16:18). For questions about confession I memorized "whose sins you forgive are forgiven them, and whose sins you retain are retained" (John 20:23). When I was a child, adults used Bible quotes to test me as a representative of my family and the Church. They hoped to confuse me.

As a result, I didn't see the Bible as friendly reading. It was difficult to understand, and it made me feel stupid. I didn't know there was such a thing as a modern translation of the Bible. I assumed that the purpose of the Bible was mainly to prove a point — and that it could be used to prove almost anything on either side of an argument. I had heard people claiming certain "truths" based on their personal interpretation of the Bible and thought those people naive at best, so it never occurred to me that I would ever want to use Scripture to prove something to myself, as an information source or for personal communication with God.

Eventually, however, I became curious about Scripture. The Christian books I was reading had Bible quotes left and right. Without ever touching my Bible, I was absorbing all sorts of information about it, and my attitude was changing without my conscious knowledge or will as I noted in these quotes soothing words for the troubled. There were words of advice for those who needed it. There were words of scolding when they were needed. There were also words of wisdom, knowledge, affirmation, challenge, and yes, even words for proving a point. I particularly noted that people in Scripture often heard things they didn't want to hear.

One day I felt compelled to read the Bible story about Paul being knocked from his horse on the road to Damascus to arrest Christians. I saw similarities between the disturbing experiences I had in church and Paul's experience on the road. I was knocked from my horse and struck blind by God. Like Paul, the direction my life was taking was out of my control. I was stunned and confused. I was a nonbeliever like Paul. We were both stubborn, so God couldn't use subtle methods with us. He had to knock us off our horses.

My desire to read that Bible story wasn't my normal "I want to read something good." I had to read it right now! So I immediately went out and bought a Bible. That afternoon a friend who had been handing me popular Christian books as fast as I could read them walked into the house and handed me a Bible! Before that day if she had given me a Bible, I would have stored it immediately on my basement bookshelf. It was creepy, especially for a skeptic.

Now I owned two modern translations of the Bible. Surely this was a sign for the hardheaded! In retrospect I wonder now why, if I wanted to read the Paul story so much, I didn't go to the shelf and take down my old translation of the Bible. It became clear: God knew what I needed because my behavior was not my normal, logical, methodical, thrifty self.

Even though I didn't know how to look up a specific story in that big fat book, I found Paul's conversion story in less than a minute — three different versions, in fact. Of course, I read them all.

Now Saul, still breathing murderous threats against the disciples of the Lord, went to the high priest and asked him for letters to the synagogues in Damascus, that, if he should find any men or women who belonged to the Way, he might bring them to Jerusalem in chains. On his journey, as he was nearing Damascus, a light from the sky suddenly flashed around him. He fell to the ground and heard a voice saying to him, "Saul, Saul, why are you persecuting me?" He said, "Who are you, sir?" The reply came, "I am Jesus, whom you are persecuting. Now get up and go into the city and you will be told what you must do." The men who were traveling with him stood speechless, for they heard the voice but could see no one. Saul got up from the ground, but when he opened his eyes he could see nothing; so they led him by the hand and brought him to Damascus. For three days he was unable to see, and he neither ate nor drank.

(Acts 9:1-9)

As my mind played over the story, I continued to see myself as being like Paul: stubborn and unbelieving, a longtime skeptic. I am outspoken like Paul. I can be cruel too. That is why God had to scare me to get me to pay attention. Suddenly I saw the uncanny occurrences that had happened to me recently in a different light. Up to that point I had avoided putting together all the wild, weird, unlikely things that had happened to me, and ignored the amazing things I had chosen to do. A year before, I had decided to return to church "for the children." Since then I had been repeatedly left trembling with fear in church. I had been reading like a madwoman any Christian book I could get my hands on and searching out anyone who would talk to me about Christ.

An Enormous Leap

I had made an enormous leap from believing that religion is a crutch for the weak and that worship and prayer are merely meaningless outward signs. That day I went from noting a string of isolated events and strange behavior to admitting that God was real and intimately involved in my life. I admitted to myself that I belonged to God, and I realized and feared his power over me. But I was seized with apprehension by one part of the story: If I am like Paul, then what am I going to be told that I must do? "Now get up and go into the city and you will be told what you must do" (Acts 9:6). I went frantically from one version of the story to another, hoping that maybe that statement would not be in them all. Each version is a bit different, but this statement is in all three. I didn't want to be told what to do. Up to this point, although I had experienced the power of God, I had not yet experienced God's love. I didn't know yet that God sends divine assistance in anything we are asked to do. I was still in the habit of thinking I needed to do everything myself. I wasn't ready to release control of my life, so this was an unnerving question: What was I going to be told that I must do?

That same day I read in John's Gospel a love letter from God to me. He told me clearly, "I came so that they might have life and have it more abundantly" (John 10:10). That was the day I experienced what it means to hear God's personal message for me in Scripture. I have no doubt God spoke to me that day. I don't understand it intellectually. I wouldn't have dared explain it to anyone, but I knew it. When I read the story of the Good Shepherd, I was one of those lost sheep.

I am the good shepherd. A good shepherd lays down his life for the sheep. A hired man, who is not a shepherd and whose sheep are not his own, sees a wolf coming and leaves the sheep. This is because he works for pay and has no concern for the sheep....I am the good shepherd, and I know mine and mine know me, just as the Father knows me and I know the Father; and I will lay down my life for the sheep. I have other sheep that do not belong to this fold. These also I must lead, and they will hear my voice, and there will be one flock, one shepherd.

(John 10:11-16)

That day I knew that the Good Shepherd had come in search of me. The Good Shepherd was willing to die for *me*. I was amazed and awed by the way God used Scripture to speak to me as an individual. I eventually learned to expect and watch for messages especially for me.

Another way the Bible spoke to me was through "Bible Roulette." I laughed at a friend as she taught me the "rules." Blindly open the Bible then read and learn what God wants to say that day. With experience I learned that often it is a love tap, a fresh insight, or a slap on the hand. A powerful example happened when Tom and I were using "Bible Roulette" to pray a decision-making novena.

Novena, from the Latin word meaning nine, refers to the nine days that the disciples were hiding in the upper room before Pentecost. In a decision-making novena you pray twenty minutes a day for nine days in succession. In the first five minutes try to empty yourself, open your mind to God, keep still, and listen. Try to let God's love permeate you. Then spend five minutes in praise and thanksgiving, using your own words or a formal prayer such as the Lord's Prayer. The idea is to pray in a way meaningful to you. For the next five minutes read a passage from one of the gospels and reflect on what God is speaking at the present moment to you. Mind you, this is not in reference to your decision. Remain open to *any* topic God chooses to discuss. Then close with five minutes of petition. In this case it was "Lord, we must decide whether to search for work overseas or to remain at home. I feel confused and uncertain. Please guide our decision." If I feel peace and harmony, I have made the right decision and should act on it. If I feel upset or agitated, then I have a troubled spirit and it means I have made the wrong decision.

Tom and I prayed each evening at the same time but in different rooms. I opened my Bible at random to John 4:34-38:

> My food is to do the will of the one who sent me and to finish his work. Do you not say, "In four months the harvest will be here"? I tell you, look up and see the fields ripe for the harvest. The reaper is already receiving his payment and gathering

crops for eternal life, so that the sower and reaper can rejoice together. For here the saying is verified that "One sows and another reaps." I sent you to reap what you have not worked for; others have done their work, and you are sharing the fruits of their work.

I reflected on the passage but never really noted any particular message for me. Then the next day I opened to the same text. That's odd, I thought. Remaining a die-hard skeptic, I double-checked the Bible to see if it automatically fell open to this page. Maybe it could be easily explained by a break in the book binding. No, it didn't automatically open there, but no matter, coincidences do happen. Even at that, it certainly made me reflect more seriously on the passage. When it happened for the third day in a row, I was overwhelmed. I couldn't explain it with book bindings or coincidences anymore. I stopped everything and raced downstairs to find Tom, who was also saying a novena. When I told him what had happened, he looked a little surprised and said, "I opened to the same passage!" Moreover, we had zeroed in on the same parts of the passage and had interpreted it in the same way. We knew that in four months we would be on our way somewhere to reap a harvest in a field we did not plant; indeed we were — East Africa.

Since my logical, rational approach to life had worked well for thirty-five years, I had approached God in the same logical, rational way. To fit my "show-me" mind, God took the initiative repeatedly to make his presence real for me. Because of who I am, I needed to use logic to convince myself that God is active in the day-to-day lives of people who aren't saintly — people like me. It took many experiences before it dawned on me that God wants me to know him. I needed logic, so he gave me logic repeatedly. Just as when I see that a cut bleeds time after time, I can assume that cuts cause bleeding even when I don't know why, so also when I experience God's action time after time in my life, I can assume that God causes this action even when I don't know why. Since I wasn't dealing with self-inflicted cuts but with an independent being, I assumed that the reason for these experiences was that God chose them. He wanted to be part of me, part of my life. God wanted a relationship with me.

When Tom and I went on a retreat sponsored by the Jesuits, we learned another way to use Scripture for meditation. This powerful prayer experience reinforced the notion that God wants to communicate with me. Sometimes it's hard to keep remembering that day after day. The experience gave me another important formalized system of meaningful communication with God. It was also a little scary because I was left with no doubt that God had used this opportunity to speak. Why is it that God's power continues to scare me? I think it's because I continue to resist complete release of my own ego. I want to hold the controls of my life.

A spiritual retreat was a new activity for our community, and we were advised to sign up quickly because surely there would be many who would want to attend. Not wanting to miss anything, I signed up immediately, along with twelve others. A Jesuit priest, whom we hadn't previously met, gave the opening statement on Friday night. "I understand that you would like to learn how to pray better. It is good that you came here this weekend to learn about prayer," he told us. We all looked at one another a little bit puzzled and wondered who had talked to this guy. We had all come to the weekend for varying reasons, but I don't believe any of us had come to learn to pray better. There wasn't much we could do about it at this point, however, so none of us complained.

The retreat leader's brief opening instructions were simple: "I understand that you are all tired, but please set aside a half hour before nine tomorrow morning for prayer. During this time read the story of Bartimaeus, the blind man in Mark 10:46-52. Read it a couple of times, then set the Bible aside and try to place yourself into the story by becoming one of the characters. You can be the

blind man himself, one of the disciples, or even one of the crowd."
It sounded a little goofy to me. I wasn't even sure I could do it. But
experience at retreats had shown me that it is better to go only on
a retreat where you trust the leaders, then try fully and whole-
heartedly to do what they ask. Otherwise, you waste your time and
theirs. So I decided I should at least try it.

By morning I had successfully avoided the exercise. It kept
popping into my mind all the way through breakfast, however. I
was feeling a little nervous because I thought my imagination
wasn't creative enough to do this exercise — especially with so
little preparation. We had been given only a few minutes of instruction with no emotional buildup to heighten the senses. At the last
minute, a half hour before starting time, I read the story twice and
set the Bible aside.

> They came to Jericho. And as he was leaving Jericho with his
> disciples and a sizable crowd, Bartimaeus, a blind man, the
> son of Timaeus, sat by the roadside begging. On hearing that
> it was Jesus of Nazareth, he began to cry out and say, "Jesus,
> son of David, have pity on me." And many rebuked him,
> telling him to be silent. But he kept calling out all the more,
> "Son of David, have pity on me." Jesus stopped and said,
> "Call him." So they called the blind man, saying to him, "Take
> courage; get up, he is calling you." He threw aside his cloak,
> sprang up, and came to Jesus. Jesus said to him in reply,
> "What do you want me to do for you?" The blind man replied
> to him, "Master, I want to see." Jesus told him, "Go your way;
> your faith has saved you." Immediately he received his sight
> and followed him on the way.
>
> (Mark 10:46-52)

Closing my eyes I imagined a dusty city in the Middle East. It
was easy to picture what Jericho must have been like centuries ago,

probably because of the many movies I had seen. A man pressed himself against the sand-colored adobe buildings that lined the dusty road. I could see he was blind. He was nervous — frightened and excited by the noise of the crowd moving down the street toward him. Then I realized that I was that man because I knew how he felt! I panicked — what was happening? Why the noise? The crowd of people? My heart was pounding. Someone shouted, "It's Jesus! It's Jesus!" I had heard about Jesus. He heals people like me! I was excited and scared. This was my chance to be whole. My mind raced wildly as I waited for him to draw near. I had to touch him, yet I was afraid to leave the security of the wall for fear of the crowd surging around me.

I planned frantically. "I will shout 'Jesus! Jesus!' when he gets close enough to hear. Surely he will come to me." As Jesus reached me, the crowd swelled. Confusion was everywhere. I tried to call out, but my throat constricted with fear. I inched along the wall following Jesus from the edge of the crowd. Jesus must have seen me because he paused on the road and looked back toward me, but he went on! He seemed to see me, but I wasn't sure. Why didn't he stop? Why didn't I shout? Then the confusion and noise began to fade. I was left clinging to the wall, bitterly disappointed. I was angry at myself for not calling out, and angry at Jesus for not stopping.

As the Spartan retreat room with the faded bedspread came back into focus, I tried to "call back" the story. I felt agitated and upset by the ending. Since it didn't end like the Bible story, maybe I did something wrong. About ten minutes seemed to have passed, and I wondered what I was supposed to do with the rest of the time. Then I looked at my watch. It was time for the meeting! I had used a half hour almost to the minute! I was confused. This was a new experience for me. Had I been transported in faith to that dusty road in Jericho?

As the group came together, the leader had us divide in half to discuss our experiences with the exercise. At first, feeling nervous and a little foolish, I didn't speak. The first person told about how Jesus had touched and healed him and about the joy and peace he felt. Now I was sure I had done something wrong! But then, to my relief, someone else related that he was in the crowd and couldn't even get near Jesus. Another person was one of the apostles. And so it went. Only one person had managed actually to touch Jesus, but no one else seemed particularly upset by the experience.

The discussion gave me confidence that I was doing it "right" even though the story hadn't ended "correctly." I also began to believe that more than just imagination was involved and hoped the next time would be more encouraging for me. The next story was from Luke, the story of Zacchaeus.

He came to Jericho and intended to pass through the town. Now a man there named Zacchaeus, who was a chief tax collector and also a wealthy man, was seeking to see who Jesus was; but he could not see him because of the crowd, for he was short in stature. So he ran ahead and climbed a sycamore tree in order to see Jesus, who was about to pass that way. When he reached the place, Jesus looked up and said to him, "Zacchaeus, come down quickly, for today I must stay at your house." And he came down quickly and received him with joy. When they all saw this, they began to grumble, saying, "He has gone to stay at the house of a sinner." But Zacchaeus stood there and said to the Lord, "Behold, half of my possessions, Lord, I shall give to the poor, and if I have extorted anything from anyone I shall repay it four times over." And Jesus said to him, "Today salvation has come to this house because this man too is a descendant of Abraham. For the Son of Man has come to seek and to save what was lost."

(Luke 19:1-10)

When I closed my eyes, I found myself clinging to a branch high in a tree as Jesus passed by. Then Jesus went directly into my house and sat in my living room with my friends. When I walked into the room, I saw them with their feet up on the coffee table, chatting and having a great time. In our house that means everyone is comfortable and having a good conversation. I looked on this cozy setting — and nobody even noticed me. I was devastated. I felt a mantle of depression settle on my shoulders as the retreat center came back into focus. I was hurting, but I was also beginning to get angry at God. Why would he do this to me?

During the discussion session which followed, I told the priests and the others in the group that I didn't like this form of prayer. In both stories Jesus didn't want to talk to me. He was avoiding me, and I didn't understand the reason. Why would a loving God bring me such pain? I was upset and had trouble containing my tears. Jesus had abandoned me. I felt isolated, lonely, and scared.

Then we had a choice of readings. One of them was the story of Jesus and the Samaritan woman at the well. (See John 4:4-30.) I chose that story because there were only two people in it. If I could be the Samaritan woman, then Jesus would have to talk to me. He would have to do some fancy footwork to avoid me! This was nonsense, of course; but still, that was the way I chose my reading. I had no trouble envisioning the village scene, since I had lived in India. As I walked toward a well in that isolated Indian village, I saw Jesus there. I recognized him instantly. I stopped before I got to the well, and Jesus saw me and started walking slowly toward me, never taking his eyes off me. The love and compassion in his eyes gripped me as I walked toward him. When he reached me, he raised his hand and touched my cheek ever so gently. His touch soothed my anger and pain.

As the scene closed, I understood that God wanted to be more intimate with me. I was avoiding a full relationship with him. I wanted to be near — but not too near. I wanted the joy, intimacy, and comfort of a loving God; but I didn't much want a God telling me what I needed to hear, a God who shows me parts of myself I don't want to face, a God who reaches inside me and knows all parts of me. I was limiting God just as I would limit a friend who could only tell me good things. God wanted to be fully real, fully alive to me.

As a result of these experiences, I came to learn how God teaches, challenges, and comforts through Scripture. I developed a curiosity about Scripture when I became curious about God. My next discovery was the wealth of resource materials that are available to help ease the way into enjoying the Bible.

Over the years I had often been amazed to hear someone recite quote after quote on a specific topic such as faith or charity. She must really know her Bible, I would think, to be able to recall so many quotes on one subject! Searching for all those topic-specific quotes must have taken hours, even days. Pretty impressive! So I was delighted when I discovered the Bible concordance, which takes a word like "faith," "tithe," or "spirit" and lists every single place that word is used in the Bible. Another discovery was the topical Bible, which is an index of related topics. If a passage is about faith, for example, but the word "faith" is not mentioned, the topical Bible will include the passage and reference. I learned to look in the back of my Bible where there is a subject index, map index, and glossary. I also discovered commentaries on specific books of the Bible. These often give the setting, customs, and beliefs of society at the time, problems of translation from the Greek or Hebrew, and other points of interest that add meaning when study and in-depth understanding is the goal. These tools not only enable a novice like me to look up quotations or topics without asking outsiders but also let me find the original quote before someone else sorts and filters what I should hear, allowing me time for reflection and cross-referencing.

It is important to know the mechanics of finding topics and

understanding the Bible, but only as those activities augment our ability to communicate effectively with God. God speaks through Scripture. The Bible guides my focus toward God rather than tying it to my needs and desires. It helps me to listen better to God, even though I don't always hear what I want to hear. I felt overwhelming desolation when I thought I was deserted by God in the Bartimaeus and Zacchaeus stories. I felt comforted and loved with the Samaritan woman story and challenged by the story of Paul. I was guided in my decision-making with the instructions to harvest where I had not planted. Prayer rooted in Scripture is rooted in the Word of God. Scripture can pave the way for two-way communication with God.

CHAPTER 3

HOW CAN I TALK WITH SOMEONE I CAN'T SEE OR HEAR?

Communication with God is an adventure. It is a relationship which develops, grows, and changes with time and experience. Think of it as a relationship with a friend. Sometimes we go to a friend for counsel; sometimes a friend comforts us. We can be angry with or feel abandoned by a friend. We can misunderstand friends and wonder why they don't speak more clearly. God speaks to us in ways that may initially seem obscure. He doesn't normally speak to us in an audible voice, so when we feel God's presence or think maybe God has answered our prayers, we tend to believe it is our imagination or a coincidence.

In this chapter I'll discuss various ways that God speaks. These methods of communication with God are not necessarily superior to others. I simply know about them because I have experienced them, and as a beginner, all this excites me. The number one thing I have learned about communication with God is that there is no "right" or "wrong" prayer. There is no "better" way to pray. I have often felt inadequate when told I should pray in a certain way. Friends advised me that I needed to use Scripture to pray "properly." They told me I must choose a specific time and place to pray each day; otherwise I wasn't doing it "right" and could not experience fully the power of prayer.

The truth is, though, that God loves us so much he seeks us out. Then it's up to us to take the opportunities he presents. I have enjoyed my exploration with God, but I wish I had understood from the first that we each have different needs and personalities in prayer, just as we do in all areas of life. These needs change with life experience and even with moods. We must continue to explore various ways of reaching God, and leave ourselves open for God to explore various ways of reaching us. Relationships with friends — and God is a friend — cannot become stagnant or the relationship dies.

God speaks to and through each one of us. The methods of communication with God described in this chapter are not intended to be limiting. This is only a small beginning, for God is far more creative at reaching us than I could ever presume to detail.

God Speaks Through Formal Prayer

Formal prayer includes any form of prayer which has a set format, including Mass and other formal church services, memorized prayers, rosaries, Liturgy of the Hours, and Stations of the Cross. For me, Mass is a powerful prayer form. I attend daily Mass regularly, carrying all my concerns to the Eucharist and placing them before God, ready to hear his instructions or consoling or whatever I need. I become one with him, then return home in peace, ready to serve him. Sunday Mass is for me a bit different, even though it has the same format. It is a community celebration of the joy of God among us. We stand together, friends and family, the community of God, praising God, reveling in his love, and finding him in one another.

A friend described her decision to begin working outside the home: "I prayed the Mass completely for myself that Monday morning before my interview. I gave the whole matter up to God. I said, 'If this is the right move, let me get the job. If it's not, then have them turn me down.' I got the job. I love it and it's been a positive growth experience for my entire family as well as for me. I have come to realize my own self-worth in a whole different perspective."

I like to pray the Lord's Prayer as part of a community of friends holding hands in a closed circle at the end of a meeting or standing as a body of believers at a formal service. It is a community prayer of unity, affirmation, willingness to serve, healing, or whatever is needed that day. Though the Lord's Prayer is a community prayer, it is also a deeply personal prayer with each line serving as the beginning of intimate communication with God.

Another friend described well the power of God at work through formal prayer: "One night while I was caring for my elderly mother, she became very disturbed and frantic. I had never seen her react this way and began to panic myself, not knowing how to keep her in the house and safe from harm. It was very late and I could not leave her to go for help. Finally, I coaxed her back into bed and suggested that we say a prayer. She lay rigid on her back with her eyes wide open, but she began to listen to the familiar prayer. We said prayers that she had heard all her life. It seemed to me that I was hearing them for the first time. I struggled to hold back the tears. In about three or four minutes, when I paused for a moment, she relaxed and turned on her side. She curled up in a childlike position on her side and said, 'I'm going to sleep now.' I could never remember a more dramatic change in a person's behavior than the one I had just witnessed."

Formal prayer can be personal or a community prayer. As

personal prayer, the repetition and familiarity of formal prayer allows our minds freedom to focus on God. It helps us center ourselves on God and release the happenings of the day, paving the way for receptivity to God's action. Formal prayer in a community setting makes us aware of God working in and through each person present and gives a sense of oneness with the community.

God Speaks Through Daily Events

As a child I had a confident faith in God's action, particularly through the Church. In high school, though, I began to doubt even the existence of God. As a senior I wrote a research paper titled "Is There a God?" in which I concluded that indeed there is a God, although I saw this God as a prime mover, not someone interested in my daily activities. During college and my early married years I prayed only occasionally. For several years after I stopped believing in prayer, Sunday Mass attendance continued as a duty only. Eventually I came to see believers as naive.

How did such a change in viewpoint develop? I could no longer believe that the judging, measuring God of my youth existed. Since I had no adult experience of God, I had nothing with which to replace this fearsome figure. As the faith of my youth crumbled, I slowly built tall, thick walls around myself. These walls protected me from what I saw as the foolish, time-consuming activities of religion and from the guilt of sin I had felt in my youth. They protected me from appearing weak by being dependent on God and religious ritual.

After my remarkable encounters with God began, each book, tape, or renewal I explored put a crack in some part of my wall. I began to question everything, to notice a strange world around me. Once when one of my newfound friends handed me a paper I needed for the Girl Scout troop I was leading, I was pleased because I had realized only moments before that I needed the information.

She responded with "God provides us what we need at just the right moment." This talk about God providing Girl Scout papers stunned me. Did she really live that way? Did she really believe it? Does God have a role in all aspects of our lives?

Since I respected this woman highly, I had to be open to the conclusion that if God cared about Girl Scouts, then he must be more active than I had suspected.

So I began to pay attention. And I observed that just the right book landed in my hand at the moment I needed to read it. The right person walked through the door and answered questions I was wondering about. I prayed for things and they happened. Others prayed for things and they happened.

At some point I began to relax and enjoy God's action in everyday events. One day I had overscheduled myself, promising to be in two places at six that evening. When I realized my situation, I chuckled to myself as I turned it over to God rather than worrying about it and getting myself in a stew. The day progressed and nothing happened until five o'clock when the phone rang. As I cradled the telephone between shoulder and ear while fixing dinner, a friend said, "Sally, the planning meeting for the camping trip has been postponed until tomorrow night, so you've got a free night." I smiled as I said "Yeah, God!" under my breath.

God's presence continued to be evident in big things and small. One night when our five-year-old daughter was sobbing with pain from an earache, I asked God to ease the pain until I could get her to a doctor. The tears stopped almost immediately.

A friend who went through those exciting early days of discovering God's surprises with me, sharing struggles in our marriages, human relationships, and child rearing, wrote, "The cement that holds me fast to God's plan are the 'God-incidents' that have happened along my journey. There have been too many little incidents that had no business working out okay, but they did. I can only explain them with the notion of God's plan being a reality."

I live day-to-day in an ongoing dialogue with God, referring problems, questions, and decisions to him. Since I often hear God through friends and neighbors, husband and children, I notice carefully what people say. Recently when I had to choose between two counselors for a family member, I first checked their backgrounds as carefully as I could. Then, before I called to interview them, I prayed that God would make it clear which one was the right choice. Since neither answered, I left my message on each of their answering machines. Only one returned my call, and I liked her immediately.

A few years ago I would have considered this a foolish way to make decisions. But I've had this "system" confirmed as not only reasonable but effective so often that it now seems imminently sensible. When I say that I prayed, I mean that I referred it to God, carrying on a loose dialogue as I would with a friend. When I make a decision, I like to "walk with it" for a day or two to give God the chance to give me peace or to deter me. It is a comfortable way for me to live. It gives me confidence, and I make fewer mistakes. I am happier.

This role of divine Problem Solver may seem to some people to trivialize God, the Supreme One. I believe, though, that God meets us where we are because he wants us to come to know him fully some day. He guides our problem-solving and even plays games with parking places and lost papers. These are natural everyday ways he can help us to come to him.

My friend describes how daily events enable her communication with God: "I became a Christian about two and a half years ago and celebrated my fortieth birthday by being baptized. Since then I have been in almost constant communication with God. The Holy Spirit has been a guide to major and minor happenings, and I guess the best way of explaining it is that the Holy Spirit uses everyday events and people and inner stirrings to get the messages across. It is quite likely that the Holy Spirit has been communicating with me this way all my life, but not until I recognized the Holy Spirit's presence in my life was I able to realize and accept the communication.

"Now I can freely ask guidance for any problem that I may have and wait and watch events unfold that tell me or show me what to do. This whole process, however, requires an absence of my own desires and ego and a total willingness to be open to the leadings."

She continued with a complicated story, with many "coincidences," of God guiding her through the selection of the proper course of action for oral surgery, including finding a good dentist in a country everyone assumes has no adequate dental care. "So I guess you could say in summary that God speaks to me through the indwelling Holy Spirit who uses all manner of events and people and just everyday occurrences."

Awareness of God creates a new way of living in which each event of the day becomes a prayer. My friend describes it beautifully: "On a regular basis I am reminded of God's love for us in everyday happenings rather than earth-shattering events. It can be something as simple as a flower blooming or a storm-blackened sky through which the sun somehow shines brightly, making the church across the street look brilliant, or as complex as a moment when I manage to keep control of an untenable situation with my daughter and settle an issue with both of us intact. I look for witnesses to God's love and power in all that I read. Such testimony is like a shot of energy to me — I need it and I look for it."

God's action in day-to-day events gives me assurance and heightens my awareness of God's presence and love in human, understandable ways. God's action encourages me and keeps me eager to develop my relationship with him.

God Speaks Through Forgiveness

After the weekend prayer retreat with the Jesuits in which I learned to pray by meditating with a Scripture story, I wanted to continue praying with Scripture. The new insights I received, as well as the new level of intimacy with God, excited me. Little did I know, though, that God was about to tell me things I didn't want to hear! I would be called to forgive an office colleague I had been battling for three years.

From the first time I walked into this man's office, there was tension between us. He wouldn't look me in the eye, smile at me, or help me out; and his surliness irritated and angered me. We reached a loose working relationship at the level of border skirmishes until we found ourselves assigned to the same office. Our border skirmishes then became full-scale war. I bad-mouthed him to anyone who would listen. Whenever possible, I avoided going near his desk. The bitterness grew until I couldn't even talk about him without hate welling up inside me.

Then one day I chose for meditation the story of the prostitute who crashed the Pharisee's dinner party and washed Jesus' feet with her tears.

A Pharisee invited him to dine with him, and he entered the Pharisee's house and reclined at table. Now there was a sinful woman in the city who learned that he was at table in the house of the Pharisee. Bringing an alabaster flask of ointment, she stood behind him at his feet weeping and began to bathe his feet with her tears. Then she wiped them with her hair, kissed them, and anointed them with the ointment. When the Pharisee who had invited him saw this he said to himself, "If this man were a prophet, he would know who and what sort of woman this is who is touching him, that she is a sinner." Jesus said to him in reply, "Simon, I have something to say to you." "Tell me, teacher," he said. "Two people were in debt to a certain creditor; one owed five hundred days' wages and the other owed fifty. Since they were unable to repay the debt, he forgave it for both. Which of them will love him more?"

Simon said in reply, "The one, I suppose, whose larger debt was forgiven." He said to him, "You have judged rightly." Then he turned to the woman and said to Simon, "Do you see this woman? When I entered your house, you did not give me water for my feet, but she has bathed them with her tears and wiped them with her hair. You did not give me a kiss, but she has not ceased kissing my feet since the time I entered. You did not anoint my head with oil, but she anointed my feet with ointment. So I tell you, her many sins have been forgiven; hence, she has shown great love. But the one to whom little is forgiven, loves little." He said to her, "Your sins are forgiven." The others at table said to themselves, "Who is this who even forgives sins?" But he said to the woman, "Your faith has saved you; go in peace."

(Luke 7:36-50)

Recalling what I had been taught by the Jesuits, I closed my eyes and became one of the Pharisee guests at this dinner party. I was annoyed by the commotion when the sinful woman arrived. She went straight to Jesus and began an embarrassing ritual, actually washing Jesus' feet with tears and perfume and drying them with her hair! I felt uncomfortable with the whole affair. I had come to the party hoping to see Jesus perform a miracle without having to follow him on the streets like an ordinary peasant. I certainly didn't come to see an emotional display by a local harlot. It was bad enough for Jesus to encourage this kind of behavior, but to use it to talk to me about forgiveness was appalling.

As the mental image of myself at the dinner party receded, my anger turned into confusion and dread as I realized that Jesus expected me to forgive my colleague and to ask for forgiveness. I was horrified. Of course, Christians are supposed to forgive and ask forgiveness. I said "I'm sorry" from time to time and truly meant it, but I doubted I could do it on this scale. Since we were planning to move soon, I knew I could walk away and never see my colleague again. I could see no advantage to healing our relationship. Besides, I wasn't sorry for my actions. I couldn't tell him I was sorry with a straight face and mean it. Jesus was asking too much and I was angry.

A week passed and the notion of forgiving my office associate kept creeping into my thoughts. I tried to pray another Scripture passage, but I couldn't even concentrate on the reading, let alone put myself into the story. I kept trying, though, selecting other stories. When nothing happened, I knew what I had to do. Jesus refused to join me because he was going to bug me until I went to my colleague and asked for forgiveness. I felt trapped.

Finally, I called my coworker on the telephone and invited him to lunch. I couldn't do it in person; the hypocrisy would be too obvious. I hoped he wouldn't accept and God would release me, since I had at least tried. Much to my chagrin, however, my nemesis accepted. During the days of waiting I practiced what I was going to say. That meal was the longest of my life. After what seemed like hours of small talk, I finally mumbled a beginning. "I, ahh…suppose you wonder why I invited you to lunch." I quickly glanced at the nearby tables to see who might be listening.

"Ahhh…you're right.…Ahhh…it is a little strange.…"

I dragged my eyes from my coffee cup to look into his blank eyes. They told me nothing. "Ahhh…I want our relationship healed before I move. I am sorry for all the things I've said and done over the years." As my companion listened in silence, my words began rolling and it got easier. It certainly wasn't hard to think of things I needed forgiveness for. "My behavior has been inexcusable. I'm sorry for all the pain I've caused and also for the unrest in the office.…" When I finally finished, I heaved a big sigh of relief. It was over. I felt no bitterness anymore. It was gone. I was at peace.

He hadn't said a word the whole time, so I was startled when he asked, "How did it all start? Did I do something wrong?" My stomach churned uneasily. I had just closed the book on years of misunderstanding, harsh words, and actions. Wouldn't enumerating specific instances of wrongdoing start the whole process again? Surprisingly, I realized that I wanted to help, not hurt him. Was this actually me wanting to be helpful? What a change!

Months after we moved, someone from the office who knew about my strained relationship with this man mentioned his name. From her silly grin I knew she expected to get a rise out of me; but I felt distance from an old situation, as though it had happened in my childhood or to someone else. The turmoil and hate were gone, and I knew then I was healed permanently.

In addition to a lesson in forgiveness, I learned to allow the Spirit to control my mind and action rather than trying to hold the controls so tightly myself. Paul says it far better than I in Romans 8:5-6:

> For those who live according to the flesh are concerned with the things of the flesh, but those who live according to the spirit with the things of the spirit. The concern of the flesh is death, but the concern of the spirit is life and peace.

The need for forgiveness is a repeated theme throughout Jesus' teaching. Jesus forgives often, even as he hangs on the Cross. The message to forgive is so central that it is bound to be evident in any communication with God. Calling us to forgive is "tough love" on God's part. When I chose to act in spite of my feelings as a response to God's call to forgive, I chose to respond to God. My pride cried out against this push to action, but I didn't need to feel sorry. I chose forgiveness; it was a decision of the mind, not of the heart. Through this call to forgiveness, God was speaking to me. I responded. This was two-way communication with God.

God Speaks by Using Us as His Instruments

When people talk about their conversion experiences, they usually speak powerfully of God communicating with people now, in modern times, and even against their will. They are often stunned and confused by these experiences, holding back and sometimes resisting what seems to be happening to them. It appears to me that in the early stages of conversion the burden of proof is with God. It's hard for unbelievers to comprehend that God is so insistent, so alive, so real. The conversion process often demonstrates that God cares enough to go to some trouble to touch us, that he is active, and expects to be operational in our lives. That takes some getting used to!

God operates actively in this world through us, his people. Few stories of God's role in individual accomplishments, both big and small, are ever told. No doubt we would all be surprised at how many activities, friendships, and services to others are inspired by God. I believe that many scientific discoveries, books, beautiful buildings, legislation, and school lessons are inspired by God. When we open ourselves to God and allow him to work in us, we get the great ideas that pave the way to that scientific discovery or piece of legislation. That is when we are brilliant beyond our understanding. That is when we behave in ways that are extraordinary for us. That is when we use our gifts more powerfully than we ever imagined possible.

For a biblical example look at the apostles, fishermen, and tax collectors cowering in the upper room after Jesus' death. These men became preachers and leaders of the most influential and long-lasting organization on earth. Look at Mary Magdalene, the town prostitute. She became a strong woman of faith and an example for us even today. In modern times Mother Teresa, a village girl from Albania, became the founder of more than two hundred inner-city centers to help the poor and abandoned. She is for our generation a model of unconditional love in service of God.

In my own life God used me as his instrument in an obvious way — to start a church community in Nairobi, Kenya. In most capital cities of the world, governments, businesses, voluntary agencies, and churches employ a nonindigenous population of international "migrant workers." Often they live a few years in one capital city, then move to another. Many in this international community fall away from a relationship with God as the numerous moves from country to country take their toll. We can integrate another culture into our view of God and worship only a few times before our energy is drained. After a time some participate, but without enthusiasm or solely from duty; many just give up formal community worship.

A Maryknoll lay missionary friend and I drank gallons of coffee as we shared our problems, assessed the problems of the church, and of course solved all the world's problems. We decided the international community needed a community celebration with songs they recognized, a homily meaningful to them, and a priest and readers from their Western culture. After scurrying around to fit all the necessary pieces together and advertising in the *American Embassy Newsletter,* we were pleased and relieved when thirty-five people showed up at the service. Excitement and anticipation reigned during the coffee hour following Mass. We heard, "When is the next Mass?" "Does it need to be so early?" We planned this as a one-time event, so we stammered and stuttered monosyllabic responses. One month later we had another service...then another...and another. The Loretto Sisters offered a beautiful chapel for our use. A priest volunteered to celebrate with us. We printed a bulletin, found a volunteer guitarist and singers, and prepared song sheets. We even gave ourselves a name, the International Faith Community.

With the monthly service established, people wanted more. So we added other activities. We collected donations for a refugee family, an orphanage, and a home for the aged. A day of reflection gave us a full day for discussion and prayer as a community. We even went camping together over the Easter holiday. Nearby lions and elephants, along with a surprise snake in one of the tents, added spice to the arrival of the Easter bunny. Soon we formed a council to organize the monthly Masses and other activities, identifying tasks: coffee hour, liturgy, bulletin, social outreach, and bookkeeping. Volunteers "just happened" to step forward when they were needed. Someone put together a hymnal with our logo on the front. Our first Christmas pageant was spectacular.

Soon the council wanted to have weekly Masses. We had no regular priest, but a priest "just happened" to offer his weekly services. A committee organized religious education for the children, then for the adults. A youth group sprang up. The community began a Christian lending library with donated books. Each Sunday the boxes of books were brought out for community perusal. Then we got a bookshelf on wheels, and eventually the community purchased books and periodicals. We organized retreats and days of prayer. Potluck dinners and pancake breakfasts became community events. As with the priest, leaders for all these events "just happened" to step forward exactly when they were needed. Panic set in when our priest was transferred to the United States, but we need not have worried. Another priest "just happened" to step forward. It looked as if our little band of musicians would fold for want of a leader when, you guessed it, one "just happened" to volunteer.

And so it went. From a small group of thirty-five, counting babes in arms, the congregation grew to a regular attendance of over two hundred in just three and a half years. These are only a few of the "just happened" stories. We would never have had that first Mass if we thought we were starting a church community. We didn't have the time! But then we didn't start that community; we were simply used, guided each step of the way.

In the early days of the community, I rushed about like the ringmaster of a three-ring circus, certain that without my services the community would fall apart. When the priest called without my asking to offer his services every Sunday, I finally understood that I wasn't the backbone; I was only God's instrument. This was God's community. He would take care of our needs as long as we allowed his action to guide us. I began to relax and watch the "coincidences" within the church with pleasure and delight. Even after we returned to the United States, the community continues to grow and to be a vibrant force. Imagine the freshness of our ideas and accomplishments if we could live our lives continually in openness to the action of God. "We" would be brilliant beyond our wildest dreams.

Establishing a church community is a big undertaking, not something we often have the opportunity to do. But it's only an example. Let's look at small day-to-day events in which God uses us as instruments if we allow it. A friend asked me to give a talk at five Sunday Masses for a special Lenten collection for the poor. "Tell us about East African life, about its people, the poor there." I felt unqualified and didn't want to draw attention to myself. Besides, I hadn't worked directly with the poor in Nairobi. We lived in a nice home and even had servants. I worked with Americans coming to Kenya as volunteers, not with poor folks. Yet I realized that if speaking on Africa was the will of God, he would give me words to say.

The request had come well in advance of the date, so I suggested to God that maybe he could find a better person for the job. In the meantime I chose not to worry about it. As the date drew closer, however, I realized I would have to speak; God wasn't going to let me off the hook easily. So a few days before the talk, I sat down at the computer and prayed for God's help. I wrote the speech with hardly a backspace or deletion and practiced it over and over during the next few days. When the day of the talk arrived, however, the last practice sounded dead and lifeless. I felt nervous; something was wrong. I prayed for God to take it out of my hands. During Mass I prayed, "Please, Lord, let me forget myself and turn it over to you." And my nervousness melted away. "I" was able to speak from memory. "I" held my audience spellbound. I had asked Tom to time it for me, but he forgot twice because he says he was so swept up in listening. Mind you, he had heard me practice at least a half dozen times! When I chose to allow God to use me as his instrument, he empowered me to speak beyond my own skill levels. He gave me confidence and boldness that I lacked.

God works through us whether or not we are aware of his action, but awareness of God's action in our lives opens new avenues that would otherwise be missed. Initially the galloping development of the community in Nairobi overwhelmed me, and I felt an enormous burden of responsibility. When I was finally aware of God's action I gained new freedom — freedom from worry and freedom to observe and enjoy the growth of the community. Another advantage to an awareness of God's action in our lives is confidence to call on God to act with us. This is what happened with the speech. Openness paved the way for God to enhance my writing and oratorical skills and certainly my self-confidence. I didn't start the church or give the speech by myself. I was an instrument of God for his purposes.

God Speaks Through Suffering

Many people begin, renew, or deepen their search for a full relationship with God during or following a time of suffering, such as the death of a family member, a serious illness, unemployment, or other tragedy. God often steps in to console or to make his presence known in time of need. Afterward the comforted person might wonder if the touch by the Divine One was just an active imagination filling a need. When the pain subsides, the curious often look for more.

Bernie Siegel, a doctor who works with cancer patients, takes it one step further. He insists that a transformation takes place because of the pain and suffering rather than in exploration and reflection after the event.

Unfortunately, most of us must suffer before we can be transformed. My wife, Bobbie, and I were sitting in the kitchen when the garbage disposal jammed. I said, "What shall I do?" She said, "Just push the reset button." So I went to God and asked, "If you're such a great creator, why didn't you give us a reset button?" God answered, "I did give you a reset button, Bernie. It's called pain and suffering." It is only through pain that we change.

(*Love, Medicine & Miracles,* Bernie S. Siegel, M.D.,
Harper & Row)

A difficult period from my own life in which I was strongly aware of God's presence and experienced a transformation came during a five-month period of unemployment. We had substantial savings, so we were not in serious financial trouble — at least not yet. The climate of unease with friends was a bigger problem. As an unemployed middle-class family, we tried to avoid talking about our plight with friends. Real live unemployed people make folks uncomfortable, even when they succeed in behaving as though everything is normal. As Christmas approached, our plans were frugal but far from empty. One evening while we were eating dinner, we heard a knock on the front door. Answering it, we found an envelope tucked inside the screen door. We broke the seal and found a hundred dollar bill. A few days later a ten dollar bill arrived in the mail — also with no name attached. We were stunned and embarrassed. We weren't poor! We could take care of ourselves!

Our pride was damaged as we saw ourselves through others' eyes. We didn't feel the way it seemed we should. We felt secure and confident during this whole time because God's presence was very real for us.

This is when I began to meet God as a real person who participated in my life. I turned easily to God during this time because he was the only effective comfort. I was open and vulnerable, so I learned many lessons I could never have comprehended in less stressful times. In giving and receiving I gained an understanding of dignity. I saw the clutter of paraphernalia in our home as excess, which does not bring or measure happiness. I compared society's evaluation of people based on their work to God's evaluation system, as found in the gospels. God used suffering as a tool to reach and to teach us.

A friend, who is probably the most gentle woman I know, was touched by God when she physically hurt someone. "When I was about eight years old, I was playing baseball on the school playground at recess. While at bat I swung and hit a good one, at the same time hitting my best friend, Suzanne, in the face with the bat. When I got to first base and looked back, she was lying on the ground and people were all around her. The place was mass confusion. I didn't pray then or think about God. All I could think about was Suzanne's father — he was short-tempered. I was sure he would not understand that it was an accident.

"We were all sent home from school while the teacher took Suzanne to the hospital. I didn't know how badly she was hurt. I told my mother what had happened and then went to my room and prayed. First I said the Our Father and then just talked to God about the problem, telling him I hadn't meant to hurt anyone and hoping it wasn't going to leave scars and ruin all her teeth. I also prayed for my parents because I thought there would be a horrible argument and misunderstanding about what had happened.

"I went outside into our yard. Suzanne's father drove up and walked toward me. I was no longer afraid but stood quietly and prepared to tell him my side of the story. Strangely, he did not ask for that. Rather, he spoke kindly and said he knew it wasn't my fault. Then he asked if he could speak to my dad. I believe that God heard my prayer, knew my fears, and somehow subtly changed this man, at least long enough to allow real communication instead of anger and misunderstanding."

When my friend was in trouble, she turned to God and was no longer afraid as she walked out to meet Suzanne's father. In the same way I was comforted and knew an unusual confidence during the long months of unemployment. We both experienced a transformation. During difficult times a comforting God brings basic change and often increases our desire for a relationship with him.

God Speaks Through Nature

We can find the thumbprint of God everywhere in creation. When we establish harmony with nature, we establish harmony with God. We can recognize God in creation in the same way that we can recognize the carpenter in the cupboard she has made or the cook in the meal he has prepared. God's presence surrounds us when we are hiking or sailing, when we are participating in God's creation. We need not be aware of God's action in creation as we sit on the riverbank with our fishing poles. We will simply sense a growing internal harmony. This harmony is harmony with God. We may only acknowledge that we feel at ease, in tune, or relaxed. My acknowledging God's presence is not what makes God present. Robert Capon captures this oneness in nature as he describes his holidays at the beach.

I take my children to the beach. On the north shore of Long Island it is a pretty stony proposition. The mills of the gods grind coarsely here; but, in exchange for bruised feet and a sore coccyx, they provide gravel for the foundation of the arts. Every year we hunt for perfect stones: ovals, spheroids, lozenges, eggs. By the end of summer there are pebbles all over the house. They have no apparent use other than the delight that they provide to man, but that is the whole point of the collection....Look at this one! Do you think it will split evenly enough for arrowheads? What color is that one when it's wet? Lick it and see. Daddy wants a big flat round one to hold the sauerkraut under the brine. Will this one do?

(An Offering of Uncles, Robert Capon,
Crossroad Publishing Company)

I also have fond memories of our holidays at the coast. I loved to snorkel on the shallow reef during low tide. My family couldn't understand why I was not frightened, and I'm not sure they ever saw me disappear without some tinge of worry. I could float for hours as I watched the coral and tropical fish present their amazing display. I was particularly fascinated with the giant sea anemone. The beauty of these colorful but stationary sea animals invites you to touch them in awe. But when you reach out to touch, you are left with a gooey substance on your hands as the folds of color seem to be sucked up into a shell that has grown into the coral. I soon learned to keep my hands to myself and just observe the action around the creatures. I came to expect a certain type of fish to be living in the folds of bright color. As I approached, the fish would lunge toward me hostilely. I learned to laugh at this harmless creature acting so bold toward me. But maybe this fish had reason to be bold. No other creature can draw near to the giant sea anemone, for its gooey surface is poisonous and serves as a trap for its next meal. I was one with nature during those hours of low tide each day.

Most of us have been touched by God through nature. When I say I feel renewed after a week of camping or snorkeling, you may say, "Come off it, Sally, anyone feels renewed after a week's relaxation. It has nothing to do with God!" But consider a week's vacation doing only things you enjoy: watching your favorite TV shows, partying, cooking, making pottery, building model airplanes, any or all your favorite activities. Now compare your sense of well-being after a week doing exactly as you want with a week at the shore or in the mountains or in any naturally beautiful setting — God's setting. I suggest that of the two, you will feel far more refreshed after a week with nature. This sense of well-being is a result of God speaking to you through nature. For this reason retreat centers generally are located in beautiful places, isolated from the city's concrete.

I'm no poet, so I can only write clichés about my sense of oneness with God while walking the reef or just sitting in the backyard listening to the locusts sing. I must turn to the Psalms for the poetry necessary to describe this phenomenon:

O LORD, your kindness reaches to heaven;
   your faithfulness, to the clouds.
Your justice is like the mountains of God;
   your judgments, like the mighty deep;
   man and beast you save, O LORD.
How precious is your kindness, O God!
   The children of men take refuge in the shadow of your wings.
They have their fill of the prime gifts of your house;
   from your delightful stream you give them to drink.
For with you is the fountain of life,
   and in your light we see light.

(Psalm 36:6-10)

God Speaks Through Art, Music, and Dance

People also find God through the great classical traditions of art, music, and dance. All the tickets to a series of ballets at the Kennedy

55

Center for the Performing Arts were sold months in advance. Handel's *Messiah* plays to packed houses every Christmas season. We read in the newspaper or hear on TV the stunning price paid at an auction for a Rembrandt or a Picasso. There can be no dollar value placed on these priceless pieces, for God participates in the talent they display. I was eighteen years old when I saw my friend dance the role of the toy doll who comes to life in *Coppelia,* and I still flash back to that thrilling night as I listen to the music more than twenty years later. God continues to speak through art, music, and dance to each generation.

Contemporary art forms are also powerful tools for communication with God. We are starting to see more liturgical dance, colorful banners, and contemporary music in our churches. Christian audiotapes, practically unheard of a few years ago, are popular gifts now. Young people enjoy Christian rock, and there are crowds of teenagers at Christian rock concerts.

Much of my own prayer of praise is through contemporary Christian music. A friend of mine tells about putting Christian music on the tape recorder one morning as the family prepared for school and work. He said nothing about it to his family. "You wouldn't believe the difference in the atmosphere," he insists. "There was no bickering or harsh words. Even the rushing seemed to be a relaxed rushing." So I tried it. Sure enough, there was a feeling of peace and ease when Christian music rather than the local radio station was playing during breakfast.

Specific individual messages can also be received through music. Sometimes a word or line from a song will "jump out and grab me." Recently, as I listened to Christian music while driving, words that reminded me of how God frees us leaped from a tape. A complete picture of a problem I had turned over to God a year before came to mind, and a gentle tap reminded me, "You keep taking back that problem. Leave it to me!" Another time when I was feeling particularly used by my family, lyrics that told of how we can live courageously in God's love caught my attention. I felt the tension drain away as I said to myself, "I'll just lean on your love for a while, Lord."

Music, art, and dance give substance to God's presence and message. Sometimes they serve to ease the heart; sometimes they are vehicles for specific messages from God. We incorporate contemporary as well as traditional art forms into church liturgies, knowing that God's presence is clearly celebrated through these mediums.

God Speaks to Each of Us

Some of the ways we can communicate with God include music, art, nature, liturgical celebrations, memorized prayer, and Scripture. God speaks through suffering and forgiveness, through daily events, and by using us as his instruments. By paying attention to God's action around us and expecting God to speak, we can enjoy the process.

There is no right or wrong way to pray. If you are in the habit of thinking that way, just put it out of your mind. God doesn't have a "system" into which we all are expected to fit. He touches each one of us in our own personal, individual way. What is right for one person may not be right for another. What works today may not work tomorrow. It is God who teaches us to pray. We give him the chance by opening the lines of communication in whatever way suits our personality, our experience, our lifestyle. Of course, prayer involves a commitment of time and effort on our part.

CHAPTER 4

CAN GOD POSSIBLY LOVE SOMEONE LIKE ME?

I believe God loves me no matter what I do, and this belief serves as a foundation for my relationship with him. I wouldn't nurture ongoing relationships with people who don't love me. I let those relationships die a natural death. Except for paid counselors, people only give counsel to those they love; and even counselors must strive for a loving relationship in order to be effective. A relationship with God is the same. When I look at the history of my understanding of God, I see that the God of my childhood was one of power and rules. I slowly let that relationship with him grow more distant. It simply never occurred to me that God loves me just as I am, that God loves me even though I don't deserve it. I began to allow my relationship with him to develop when God finally convinced me of his love. Is this imagination at work? I don't think it is.

Whenever I have doubts about what someone is telling me, I go to Scripture to check what I'm hearing. God has given us this tangible system of cross-checking the confusing messages that society, our Church, and even he sends to us. In Scripture God's love for us comes up over and over. I always thought the God of the Old Testament was fierce and not very loving. But even in the Old Testament God tells his people that he loves them. Remember that Gentiles, which includes most of us, are full heirs to all the promises that God made to the Israelites (see Ephesians 3). Read the Old Testament. A message of love is spoken to each of us as heirs of the Israelites.

It was not because you are the largest of all nations that the LORD set his heart on you and chose you, for you are really the smallest of all nations. It was because the LORD loved you and because of his fidelity to the oath he had sworn to your fathers....The LORD, your God, is God indeed, the faithful God who keeps his merciful covenant down to the thousandth generation toward those who love him and keep his commandments.

(Deuteronomy 7:7-9)

Notice the last part of the statement — "those who love him and keep his commandments." That is disconcerting for me since I don't view myself as always keeping his commandments. I sometimes think: Do I love God as I should? Do I love my neighbor as I was commanded? What about the Ten Commandments? Sure, I didn't kill anybody, but what about the damage I did to the ego of my daughter or my friend? Did I put another god first? It is true that I didn't bow down to the statue in Grandiose Mall, but what about all the goods in the stores? Are they my idols? Am I a slave to the accumulation of the world's goods? Look at my TV, VCR, dishwasher, and computer! Look at my clothes closet! So much stuff! Obviously I don't really obey his commands, so God must not really love me.

So I say to myself, "I think I'll check further in the Bible. Surely there is more evidence that 'God loves me!' "

> Great and awesome God, you who keep your merciful covenant toward those who love you and observe your commandments.
>
> (Daniel 9:4)

And so it goes again. I keep checking and checking, and still there is always that big "if." *If* you obey his commandments. *If* you love him.

Then I check the New Testament because it was Jesus who began preaching about love. It was Jesus who held up love as a way of life. I find in John:

> "This is my commandment: love one another as I love you. No one has greater love than this, to lay down one's life for one's friends. You are my friends if you do what I command you."
>
> (John 15:12-14)

Indeed in both Old and New Testaments, love is tied to a big "if." We must obey his commands. It would be an incomplete message if God didn't challenge us to follow him fully. God has to insist that we follow his commands and that we love him and others. If he doesn't challenge us, there is no backbone to God's message or to our call to be fully participating Christians. Paul beautifully summarizes this call when he says, "I...urge you to live in a manner worthy of the call you have received" (Ephesians 4:1).

On the other hand, if God loves us with a string of "ifs," and we are to love others with more "ifs," then there would be no depth or fullness to the message. As sinners we would be so discouraged we would give up if we needed to worry constantly about whether we are good enough for God to love us. Our spiritual life would be a disaster and our power as Christians would fall flat if we had to run around trying to convince ourselves or the world that God loves us.

It's one thing to be told that God loves me; it's quite another to experience God's love. I can see now why I parted ways with that fearsome God who had a code I had to obey or be severely punished. In retrospect it is clear I was following rules in an attempt to win God's love, although I didn't realize it at the time. My lack of belief in God's love for me was an obstacle which had to be overcome before I could develop a relationship with him. God shook me with his power and even gave me gifts of knowledge and prophecy. But still I needed confidence in his love to move on.

Eventually the story of the Prodigal Son brought me confidence in God's love, breaking down the barriers that were holding me frozen in uncertainty. I finally became convinced that God loves me, even though I know for sure that I am not good enough. The story from Luke 15 follows:

Then he said, "A man had two sons, and the younger son said to his father, 'Father, give me the share of your estate that should come to me.' So the father divided the property between them. After a few days, the younger son collected all his belongings and set off to a distant country where he squandered his inheritance on a life of dissipation. When he had freely spent everything, a severe famine struck that country, and he found himself in dire need. So he hired himself out to one of the local citizens who sent him to his farm to tend the swine. And he longed to eat his fill of the pods on which the swine fed, but nobody gave him any. Coming to his senses he thought, 'How many of my father's hired workers have more than enough food to eat, but here am I, dying from hunger. I shall get up and go to my father and I shall say to him, "Father, I have sinned against heaven and against you. I no longer deserve to be called your son; treat me as you would treat one of your hired workers." ' So he got up and went back to his father. While he was still a long way off, his father caught sight of him, and was filled with compassion. He ran to his son, embraced him and kissed him. His son said to him, 'Father, I have sinned against heaven and against you; I no longer deserve to be called your son.' But his father ordered his servants, 'Quickly bring the finest robe and put it on him; put a ring on his finger and sandals on his feet. Take the fattened calf and slaughter it. Then let us celebrate with a feast, because this son of mine was dead, and has come to life again; he was lost, and has been found.' Then the celebration began. Now the older son had been out in the field and, on his way back, as he neared the house, he heard the sound of music and dancing. He called one of the servants and asked what this might mean. The servant said to him, 'Your brother has returned and your father has slaughtered the fattened calf because he has him back safe and sound.' He became angry, and when he refused to enter the house, his father came out and pleaded with him. He said to his father in reply, 'Look, all these years I served you and not once did I disobey your orders; yet you never gave me even a young goat to feast on with my friends. But when your son returns who swallowed up your property with prostitutes, for him you slaughter the fattened calf.' He said to him, 'My son, you are here with me always; everything I have is yours. But now we must celebrate and rejoice, because your brother was dead and has come to life again; he was lost and has been found.' "

(Luke 15:11-32)

What always struck me about the story of the Prodigal Son was that it seemed to me the older son, who always did the right thing, got a bad deal, while the younger son came back after spending his father's fortune expecting to live off the family again. As a thrifty person, I have no patience with the behavior of the spendthrift son. When the father was begging the older son to join the festivities, I had always glossed over, or never noticed, his words, "My son, you are here with me always; everything I have is yours." I needed to know that the older son got his full reward. Once this was pointed out to me I could begin to look seriously at the whole story.

One day I listened to this story on an audiotape as I did my household chores, carrying the tape recorder from the kitchen to the bedroom to the laundry room. I was folding clothes when I was suddenly overwhelmed with God's love for me. God actually loves me, Sally. He loves me even though I sometimes doubted his very existence. I often resented him; sometimes I even hated him. Suddenly I could see the ways he had been trying to convince me of his love. I understood that I am the child in the story who breaks my Father's heart. I realized that my Father always loves me no matter how bad I am or how far I stray. I recognized that my Father stands on the road each day watching and waiting for me to return. It doesn't matter that I have denied him, that I have hurt him, that I have broken his commandments. Still he calls for a celebration when I come back.

As a parent I was forced to think about what my children would have to do before I stopped loving them. If they stole from me, would I still love them? If they told me they didn't need me ever again and walked out the door, would I stop loving them? If they didn't contact me for ten years, would I stop loving them? If I didn't approve of their occupations or their lifestyles, would I stop loving them? No. I would never stop loving them. The father in the story loved this way. So God loves me just as much as I love my children.

As I continued to reflect on the story, however, I had to admit that if my daughter behaved as badly as the prodigal son I would expect — no, demand — an apology. I would not look on her with pity as the father in the story did. I would be angry. I certainly would give her a proper lecture about her behavior, and probably would set up a payback system or at least charge rent. I'm not so sure I would put her on my insurance policy or enroll her in college. I would certainly not open that special bottle of wine I was saving, nor would I call in the neighbors, my family, and friends for a party. Rather, I would be embarrassed that my child treated me so callously and make excuses to my friends about why I even allowed her to come back home. My Father's love is blind! It appears that he loves me even more than I love my own children!

> For God so loved the world that he gave his only Son, so that everyone who believes in him might not perish but might have eternal life.
>
> (John 3:16)

At times I have tried to earn my way into God's favor. During my early upbringing I tried to follow the rules so God would love and reward me. Later I decided to go to church so God would reward my children with his love and care if they needed it. In more recent years I planned to go to Mass, read Scripture, say the rosary, attend group meetings for spiritual renewal, visit the sick, give more money to the Church and to the poor, be kinder to my children, communicate better with friends and my husband, and even lose weight for God. When I set goals like this, they often become burdens and cause for resentment. They are also unnecessary, since nothing can separate us from God's love. Let's look at Romans 8:

> What will separate us from the love of Christ? Will anguish, or distress, or persecution, or famine, or nakedness, or peril,

or the sword?...No, in all these things we conquer over-whelmingly through him who loved us. For I am convinced that neither death, nor life, nor angels, nor principalities, nor present things, nor future things, nor powers, nor height, nor depth, nor any other creature will be able to separate us from the love of God in Christ Jesus our Lord.

(Romans 8:35, 37-39)

Confidence in God's love has changed my life. I go to Mass, read Scripture, pray, and so on; but I don't regard these things as goals, attempts to earn God's favor. They are ways for me to know God better and to be near him. Praying is an exciting opportunity to throw open the lines of communication. It isn't an "earn-your-way" system; rather, God gives me the opportunity to be near him. I won't turn down that gift, for it brings permanent love, strength, and security that can't be gained any other way.

God Wants to Guide Us

You may remember the exact moment you accepted God's love, or it may have been a slowly evolving realization. Confidence in God's love comes to us in different ways. I asked a friend when she made her leap of faith, and she responded, "I think that I gradually eased myself into the belief that God loves me rather than making a 'leap' as you put it. That is a difference in our personalities, isn't it, Sally? You leap and I sort of ease into a spot! To tell you when I finally was convinced that I am loved by God would require a review of my life. I really can't pinpoint the time."

I took a leap, and my friend eased into belief of God's love. Maybe you're not yet convinced. If not, that day will come, because God's love is so great that he will persist in his effort to convince you of his love. In Isaiah, God says,

Can a mother forget her infant,
　be without tenderness for the child of her womb?
Even should she forget,
　I will never forget you.
See, upon the palms of my hands I have written your name;
　your walls are ever before me.

(Isaiah 49:15-16)

He has also promised to guide us.

I will instruct you and show you the way you should walk;
　I will counsel you, keeping my eye on you.

(Psalm 32:8)

In the New Testament Jesus urges us to believe that he loves us, even luring us with his love and his promises.

"Come to me, all you who labor and are burdened, and I will give you rest. Take my yoke upon you and learn from me, for I am meek and humble of heart; and you will find rest for yourselves. For my yoke is easy, and my burden light."

(Matthew 11:28-30)

Jesus promised to send the Holy Spirit when he leaves.

"I will ask the Father, and he will give you another Advocate to be with you always, the Spirit of truth....I will not leave you orphans; I will come to you."

(John 14:16-18)

Another friend wrote, "Until I was in my early thirties, I considered myself a normal, faithful Catholic who attended Mass and the sacraments as required. I never heard of a person having a personal relationship with Jesus or receiving daily guidance from him or being deeply in love with him and aware of his love in a real sense.

"Because several people, whom I trusted, insisted that all of the above were true for them, I decided to seek it for myself. I began doing what my friends said they did, talking to Jesus as if he were sitting beside me.

"I told him of my doubts about all of this but admitted it sounded wonderful — if it were possible. I told him I would like to have a God who cared about small, unimportant things. A God I could really talk to…and listen to. A God who had time to be with me. I told him I would love to follow his guidance if he could show me he was alive and wanted to be part of my life. But I also told him I needed to be sure…to know he was answering me.

"At that point, God overwhelmed me with his presence. He removed every trace of doubt from my mind. I no longer just knew about him — I met him face-to-face. I was aware only of his glory and his all-consuming and unconditional love for me."

When God says he will guide us and be with us, he means it. Sometimes we choose to listen to God's guidance, and sometimes we don't. But whether we listen or not, he still guides us. In the same way, when I was younger I received good advice from my mother and father. Sometimes I chose to take the advice and sometimes I didn't. When I didn't, they didn't stop loving me, and they didn't stop giving me the advice.

For lots of reasons I sometimes misunderstood my parents' counsel. Maybe I didn't listen closely enough. Maybe I didn't put it into the context of my whole life or combine it with other advice I had received. Sometimes I didn't believe it or didn't want to believe it, and so on. With God's guidance it is the same.

Now I look at my role as a parent. I give advice regularly to my children. Mostly it is good advice, given because I love them and don't want them to make mistakes or to be unhappy. I don't want them to have unnecessary anxiety. I won't stop loving them when they don't take my advice; on the other hand, I won't stop giving advice. God, my perfect Parent, counsels me because he loves me. He loves me even more than I love my children. He told us:

> "What father among you would hand his son a snake when he asks for a fish? Or hand him a scorpion when he asks for an egg? If you then, who are wicked, know how to give good gifts to your children, how much more will the Father in heaven give the holy Spirit to those who ask him?"
>
> (Luke 11:11-13)

A primary lesson I received as a child and carried into adulthood was that if I am good, then God loves me; most of the time, though, I am not good enough. Old attitudes die hard. Through God's persistence I was finally able to accept his love and understood that it was not dependent on my actions. Only when I accepted God's love was I able to participate fully in two-way communication with him. When I'm sure I'm loved, I can feel secure even in the bad times. Now that I'm sure of God's love, I can and must step forward to do the hard things as well as the exciting things. Now that I'm sure I'm loved, I am more confident and courageous. I am more bold to act in new ways.

CHAPTER 5

IS THIS STUFF REALLY FROM GOD?

It is logical and sensible to wonder if an idea or feeling you have is really from God. After all, you've had hunches all your life; maybe it is just intuition. You've probably learned to be skeptical when you hear claims that God sent a message to someone. Often the message seems self-serving or highly unlikely. Skepticism then leads to doubt that God is really communicating with anyone. The authenticity of messages from God is a subject that should be brought out of the closet and addressed in a practical straightforward way.

No matter how specifically and confidently I write down the tests I use for true communication with God, there are times when I wonder how much of an idea is mine and how much is God's. I distrust others on this matter, and I observe carefully in conversations and books when someone states that he or she experienced God.

Having always been a doubter, when I realized that God was communicating with me, I had to begin making new kinds of judgments about my thoughts, feelings, and ideas. It was scary at first. I was too embarrassed to ask questions, but I needed to know when it was God and when it was me. I make that judgment better now and live with greater peace than I did a few years ago because, given enough time, I can usually tell the difference. I automatically eliminate stray ideas more quickly now. I wait more patiently when I am not sure, confident that God will straighten out my thinking in due course. I write these "keys" to knowledge knowing that God cannot be categorized or manipulated. If he could, the excitement of a relationship with him would be lost, and we would quickly lose interest. Generally, faith is necessary to understand that God is interacting with us. I say "generally" because God wants so much to be a part of us he often initiates communication with a non-believer in powerful ways, as he did with Saul of Tarsus on the road to Damascus (Acts 9:1-9). Sometimes this communication is the beginning of faith — as it was for me. Other times the person is tempted to believe that it can be real, possibly does for a while, but eventually dismisses it as imagination.

Amid the many confusing signals I thought might be from God but suspected were my overactive imagination, I developed a system of "tests" which helped sensitize me to God. Each one of the methods I'll discuss is appropriate within an ongoing friendship with God. I expect experience to improve the reliability of my current tests. You'll recognize many of them as previously mentioned, but they should be enumerated because they are important to the confident believer as well as the skeptic.

Use Everyday Communication Skills

In any conversation with a friend, we use different methods to understand the importance and accuracy of their suggestions, taking into account our own moods and background knowledge. We hear the words as well as listen for tonal clues. We notice facial expression and body language. We automatically refer to the characteristics, mind-set, and behavior patterns of that person. We ask questions and wait for a response. Sometimes we ask a friend for advice. Communication with God uses these same techniques. We must keep still and listen, ask questions and wait for a response, notice moods and behavior patterns. Communication skills and depth of friendship grow hand in hand. Think of the difference in depth of friendship possible with a six-year-old compared to a sixteen-year-old. It takes practice to develop communication skills with friends and family — and with God.

Most everyday communication techniques are valid with God, but because communication with God is not normally audible — one of our primary methods for communication — it's easy to become confused. We need to open ourselves to new ways of "hearing" God without shutting down our normal human systems.

Notice Feelings, Thoughts, and Changes

God uses feelings and thought processes as a primary way to reach us. I learned to pay attention to my feelings — negative and positive. If I experience a drastic change of heart or mind, I try to be especially alert. A sense of urgency sent me to the story of Paul's conversion. Feelings of equanimity encouraged me to continue listening to Christian music during breakfast. Feeling isolation and distance from God, I asked my colleague for forgiveness. Sometimes feelings give clear signals, but sometimes the signals are confusing.

I questioned other people who talk about God acting in their lives. How do you know it's God? Usually they reply, "I just knew." "I felt sure." "I would never do anything like that on my own." A friend who began giving things away to lighten the burden of possessions in his life said, "My life was devoted to acquiring more and more. I know it's the Lord telling me to get rid of stuff because it's not my normal course of action. It must be God."

Another common reply was "I didn't realize it was God working until it was over." An alcoholic friend described his time following treatment at a rehabilitation center. "I believe I have been healed. I didn't know it at the time but I do now, because I have no desire for liquor. It's like people who have never tasted caviar and then are told that they can never have it. They don't miss it. Other alcoholics usually have to keep busy to keep their minds off alcohol. I feel like I've never tasted it."

When I asked a friend how she knew when God was speaking to her, she put into a few words what I have stretched out over many pages: "Usually it involves changes in feeling: (1) feeling at peace; (2) feeling stronger, more sure; (3) feelings of breaking a barrier; (4) feeling different about oneself; (5) feeling differently about another; (6) feeling calm in the middle of chaos."

Using feelings as a test for God's presence can make us strange and vulnerable in our "prove-everything" world. It is difficult to trust feelings, particularly when they are confusing. For example, I felt confused as our daughter prepared to go to college. Gradual independence from us began when she started to walk, but this seemed like an enormous leap! I tried to use feelings to guide me toward a new role as a parent. It included such daily decisions as how much financial support should we provide? Should I make her dentist appointment before she goes? Should I go to the bank with her to open her first checking account? Because I had been conditioned to protect her since she was born, my feelings were mixed up. I seem able to use feelings with more clarity when presented with a fresh idea, one not so conditioned by a long history. And when I use feelings as a guide, I need to know myself, my weaknesses, and my strengths.

Many times God guides us to new ideas and changes that alone we would never consider. We can recognize much of God's action through our feelings: feelings of rightness, wrongness, excitement, peacefulness, agitation. We can dismiss these feelings as passing notions of our own creation or choose to live in awareness that God often uses feelings to speak.

Is It Good?

This test for the authenticity of a message from God is quick and can easily be used on all communications. God would never have us do anything that is evil or that would hurt someone.

The Bible gives us four different versions of the life of Christ. Because we have a good idea of how Jesus would behave in any given circumstance, we can judge if an action fits with the way he would act. This test alone can help us disregard some messages: If we are "called" to do evil, we can be sure that it is not of God. We should always ask ourselves, "Would Jesus do something like that?" "Is it like Jesus?"

A Christian friend asked me to pray for her because she was having trouble preparing a talk on mercy to give at a conference. On my way to Mass I prayed, "God, have you got any useful ideas for Susan? She's looking for your input." Suddenly I had the idea that she should include forgiveness of self in her talk. I could see how I often judge myself harshly for the pain I cause in others. Since I have trouble forgiving myself, it makes it hard for me to understand God's forgiveness and mercy. Was this a message from God? I don't know. Maybe it was a message for me, not for Susan. After Mass I told Susan this idea for her talk preparation. Why? The idea came after praying. It is good stuff. It can't possibly hurt anyone. She could use it or discard it, whichever seemed appropriate. I knew that Susan would approach her task prayerfully and include my "pearls of wisdom" as only one bit of information.

It wasn't necessary to use other methods to confirm my message for Susan because of its simplicity and the person affected. No, it couldn't hurt anyone. It was good.

Is It to My Advantage?

Unless evil is clearly evident, I usually use additional methods for discernment. A second test is to ask, "Is it to my advantage?" This one can be tricky because God often suggests activities which are to our advantage. He wants the best for us, so he nudges us into activities which help us. So just because something is to our advantage doesn't mean it is not of God; but it does flag it as a suggestion to be carefully observed. Give God an opportunity to let you know if you have misunderstood his instructions. Allow time for confirmation from another source, think about it, pray. If it is truly from God, it won't go away. It will become clearer and more refined. There is one thing to remember with all messages and tests, though. God doesn't run on our human timetable.

We had to be cautious when Tom got a job offer after four months of unemployment. Our instincts were to accept immediately. We were eager to be out of the unemployment ranks and would naturally be excited to find work. The offer seemed perfect and definitely to our advantage. But was this the work he was supposed to be doing? To slow down the process and to give God a chance to confirm or deny what seemed to be a wonderful gift, Tom told his prospective employer that he would give them his answer in ten days. We began to pray. He did take the job, and indeed it was right for the whole family. Just because the job offer was to our advantage did not exclude it from being God's will, but it did signal us to move slowly to be alert.

If a message, a gift, or an instruction from God seems self-serving, we must use other tests for authenticity, but we don't need to dismiss the communication completely. God wants us to be challenged. He wants us to grow and to be happy. We must be careful, though, since the ego can easily shape and bend God's message. We must redouble our efforts at discernment when a message seems to be personally advantageous.

Does It Stand the Test of Time?

When in doubt, wait. Sometimes when I take the time to let ideas or thoughts "rest on my mind," they just slip away. This happens even with ideas I'm excited about or with responses which seem to be the answer to prayer. Weeks later I might remember it as one of my "bright" ideas.

Sometimes an idea seems too hard, or it seems outrageous. Waiting allows God time to plant a seed and then nourish it. It also gives us time to get accustomed to some of his more dramatic plans.

Currently I am working on one of the seeds God planted months ago. I don't know yet how it will work out, but I can see clearly the planting, nourishing, and pruning of the initial idea. I got the seed of an idea that going back to graduate school to study theology or spirituality would prepare me for the perfect job God has in mind for me. What that job is I didn't know then, and I still don't know. Initially, graduate school seemed outrageous and more hard work than I wanted to tackle.

When I began thinking about going to school, I wrote to various graduate-study programs only to learn I needed a background in Greek and Hebrew to be eligible for theology. So I began to look at other programs, asking continually for guidance and the prayers of others. Although I was confused, my interest was definitely piqued. Then I got sidetracked into writing this book and wondered if it was my personal "graduate school." I was sure I didn't belong in Greek and Hebrew philosophy and theology just to prepare for graduate school. When I found another program that interested me, applications and testing schedules overtook my writing schedule for a time. Still I continued to write, to wait, and to see what would happen to my graduate-school idea.

Often I don't understand why God wants me to do something, and I don't always see concrete results when I am finished. It is possible that I won't end up in school or with a job or a published book, but maybe that wasn't the purpose at all. The whole exercise of searching for and applying to programs and jobs forced me to analyze my strengths and weaknesses and to decide what I want to do "when I grow up." It made me analyze honestly just how I would mix my home, marriage, studies, or work successfully. Maybe the whole purpose of the exercise is to leave myself open to God's will, exploring all the avenues he opens, confident that he will bar the gate to the wrong ones.

The idea of graduate school hasn't gone away. It is still alive and kicking. Maybe it was only a seed planted and needing my test of time to mature. But I have more peace now about the professional part of myself than I have had for the past twenty years, and I feel comfortable with whatever happens. These feelings serve as an indicator of the direction God is leading me.

Waiting allows time for an idea to mature. When an idea is from God, it will not just fade away. It may change and develop, but it will not disappear.

Does Enthusiasm Develop?

If God wants us to do something, he gives us enthusiasm for it. For example, for a time I considered going into the property-management business. During the test of time I not only expected enthusiasm to develop, I wanted it to because property management seemed so right for Tom and me. I gathered all the information and consulted with people working in the field. All the while I discussed the matter with God, suggesting that this really was right. "Hey, God, this is a great idea. It's perfect for Tom and me. I'll build up the business, then after a few years Tom and I can work together! Let's get with it!" When the enthusiasm I waited for never came, all the materials I had gathered were relegated to file number 802.3, Property Management, located far to the back of my file cabinet. Who knows? Maybe the day will come when, indeed, it will be right.

Enthusiasm was my indicator for many of the activities within the Church community in Nairobi, such as the education program for the children. I felt only a little interest in the beginning, but I saw my enthusiasm develop as I began gathering information. The enthusiasm test has pushed me into some activities and diverted me from others. It is especially useful for long-term projects.

Does a Sense of Urgency Develop?

I often use the "sense of urgency" test for actions I feel God has instructed me to do. These are generally things I wouldn't do on my own — usually because there is a certain amount of risk involved or it seems foolish. When the idea comes, I begin to form the action in my mind. Then I wait. Sometimes a sense of urgency develops, and I know I must act. This test saves me from impulse actions. At the same time I am not stopped from doing the outlandish things God sometimes wants done.

For example, recently I felt an urge to send a set of Christian tapes to a family friend in the hospital. John had participated in prayer at meals in our home, but we had never discussed our beliefs. I tried some of my standard tests, but the answers were not obvious. (1) Is it good? It seems so, but not if John becomes antagonistic or feels pushed and cuts off communication. Cramming God down someone's throat is not helpful to anyone. (2) Does it hurt anyone? It seems it couldn't hurt, but if he becomes angry it could impede the healing process and negate my usefulness as a friend. (3) Is it to my advantage? It doesn't seem to be because I don't want to do it. An overture like this could end our friendship. I didn't want to take the chance.

What should I do? Wait. I must give God the chance to let me know that I have understood correctly — or misunderstood. I must "walk with it" a few days.

Several days after I put the idea on "hold," my daughter announced that she was going to the hospital. Then the tape idea began to churn. I knew I had to package the tapes with a nonthreatening cover letter. In addition to what John would think, I needed to consider my daughter. It would embarrass her to be the courier for this package. I even considered gift wrapping the package so she wouldn't know what it was but decided that would be deceitful. She told me later she felt foolish because John called himself an atheist, and it seemed ridiculous at best to take him Christian tapes. She did it anyway to humor her mother. Much to everyone's surprise, however, John listened to the tapes and even shared them with a friend. The time lapse between idea and action was about a week.

Although I do act on my own ideas, I only want to do some activities if they are God's plan for me. They will go better if they are God's will. Others I don't want to do but must do if they are God's will. It's easy to be taken in by an impulse response. Waiting slows down the process so we can see God's action on the issue. Sometimes he gives us an overwhelming sense of urgency to spur us to action.

Do I Feel at Peace?

Living in a continuing effort to act according to God's will brings more peace and freedom from worry. We don't necessarily do easier things, and we may even find ourselves doing the same things but in a different way. Life becomes a collaborative effort as we grow in areas we had previously neglected. Life is more interesting and exciting. We begin to measure accomplishments by a different standard. We can put aside the world's typical measuring system — money and prestige — and replace it with the rightness of a given activity for us.

When we feel at peace we know we are on the right track. But lack of peace can also serve as an indicator of God's will. For example, last fall we enrolled our twelve-year-old daughter in a special school for the deaf. She has a severe hearing loss and although she has managed in regular classrooms, she was having trouble both academically and socially at school. That first week of school was a nightmare. She hated the new school, and I ached for her. A friend visited me and, after hearing my story, she said, "Sally, you must have talked to God about this. If God has assured you that this is the right thing to do, then you should have no fear of your decision." I realized then I made the decision based only on logic. I visited the school, interviewed teachers, and checked with the hearing specialists; but I did not ask God what to do. I rethought my decision as I took it to God in prayer. In the end I reenrolled her in public school. It was a difficult year for her, but she dealt effectively with each problem as it came. Had I paid attention to my "Do-you-feel-at-peace?" test, this traumatic experience could have been avoided.

The peace test can also be confusing at times — particularly if we're finally settling a longstanding problem or decision. We may think we're feeling peace when what we are actually feeling is relief. Turmoil is created simply by the need to decide, which has nothing to do with the decision itself. Tension is released when the decision is finally made or the problem solved. Release of tension is not peace, however.

This happened when Tom and I decided to quit presenting marriage retreats after returning to the United States. We vacillated. "It would be good for us." "It is too much work." "We have much to offer." "It is a big-time commitment." For the few days following our decision I didn't exactly feel peaceful, but I didn't feel tied up in knots either. What I felt was relief, since we had been discussing the decision for months. I learned to be wary of the difference between relief and peace.

God gives or withholds inner peace to help us to know when we are heading in the right direction.

Ask for Signs

The practice of asking for signs, miracles for the purpose of confirming faith, can be found in Scripture. God gives signs when he is asked, but only for really important reasons. There is a risk involved, for if a requested miracle doesn't happen, our faith is tested more severely than if we had not asked. Gideon, in the reading that follows, certainly didn't hesitate to ask for a sign. To "put out a fleece" has become an idiomatic phrase for a sign.

Gideon said to God, "If indeed you are going to save Israel through me, as you promised, I am putting this woolen fleece on the threshing floor. If dew comes on the fleece alone, while all the ground is dry, I shall know that you will save Israel through me, as you promised." That is what took place. Early the next morning he wrung the dew from the fleece, squeezing out of it a bowlful of water. Gideon then said to God, "Do not be angry with me if I speak once more. Let me make just one more test with the fleece. Let the fleece alone be dry, but let there be dew on all the ground." That night God did so; the fleece alone was dry, but there was dew on all the ground.

(Judges 6:36-40)

There are also examples of signs from God in the New Testament. God gave Zachariah, the father of John the Baptist, a sign when he had trouble believing that he and his wife, Elizabeth, who was well past her childbearing years, would have a child. Zechariah was far more general than Gideon in his request for confirmation. Gideon gave God the specifics he wanted in the sign. Zechariah simply asked for a confirmation of faith.

> Then Zechariah said to the angel, "How shall I know this? For I am an old man, and my wife is advanced in years." And the angel said to him in reply, "I am Gabriel, who stand before God. I was sent to speak to you and to announce to you this good news. But now you will be speechless and unable to talk until the day these things take place...." When he came out, he was unable to speak to them, and they realized that he had seen a vision in the sanctuary. He was gesturing to them but remained mute.
>
> (Luke 1:18-20, 22)

When I visited John, the hospitalized atheist friend I had given the Christian tapes to, we used both types of requests for signs. I, like Zechariah, made a general request for confirmation, asking God to show his presence to John. John, on the other hand, asked for a specific sign, a cross.

My visit to the hospital that day began in the usual lighthearted vein. We seldom discussed anything very serious, so John seemed strangely nervous as he said, "You know, Sally, you would be surprised to know that I have always been envious of you and Tom." I couldn't imagine what he was going to say during the long, awkward silence. "People who can believe in God with confidence, as the two of you do, seem so much happier than the rest of us. I have accepted God on two different occasions and after two weeks it just went away. Now for me to believe, I need proof that there is a God."

Dumbfounded, I paused and prayed quickly, "This one is yours, God!" Then I impulsively declared, "John, tell God that you need proof."

He was surprised. "Nobody ever told me that before!" he said. "They always told me that I just have to have faith."

I suggested we pray together, and he accepted my hand with restraint. He was damp with perspiration and obviously uncomfortable. Under the circumstances I bowed my head and said a quick prayer, "Lord, you promised that when two or more are gathered in your name, you will be there; so we know that you are here. Please let John know that you are real. He is having trouble believing it. Amen." I went home wondering what would happen.

On my next visit John told me this story: "That night I prayed and prayed. I begged God to prove himself to me. I asked him to show me with a cross. I had a dream. Well, it seemed like a dream; but I'm not sure. I saw a beautiful cross with the points going on and on forever. It was set in a medallion with colored lights behind it. Then I saw Jesus in the dream, and believe it or not he was wearing a leather jacket!"

God gave John his cross and an image of Jesus individualized to suit his personality and lifestyle. God did, indeed, give a sign, a miracle for the purpose of confirming faith.

Signs are sometimes unsolicited. My mother received a sign when she was deciding whether or not to remarry after being widowed for eleven years. "I was trying to make up my mind about whether to marry Herb or not. I decided to say a novena. You told me I could ask for a sign, but I didn't believe in asking. If God wanted to give me a sign, he would, I thought. On the last day, I said the prayer in the morning. That afternoon I was at the pool and a Vogue motor home like Herb's (there are not many Vogues) drove up. A man built like Herb got out (there aren't many men built like Herb). He had on a cowboy hat and boots like Herb wears. Just for a second I felt so happy to see him. Of course, I quickly realized that it wasn't Herb; so I figured that was my sign."

Signs can be solicited or unsolicited. They can have specific parameters in which God is expected to respond, like John asking for a cross or Gideon requesting wet wool. Signs can also be general requests, like my prayer for John's assurance of God's reality or Zechariah's request for confidence in the angel's message.

Ask Another Christian to Pray

Another way to confirm communication with God is to ask another Christian to pray. Prayer should not solely involve listening to the inner self. It should also look toward the community of God.

Reliance on community was the first lesson God taught Paul at his conversion to Christianity. After he was knocked from his horse and blinded, he had to depend on his travel companions to escort him to Damascus. Three days later the Christian Ananias went to Saul, "Saul, my brother, the Lord has sent me, Jesus who appeared to you on the way by which you came, that you may regain your sight and be filled with the holy Spirit" (Acts 9:17). Christ, by his very lifestyle within the community of the apostles, encourages us to operate not in isolation but as part of a body of believers.

During the months after moving back to the United States I felt I was racing up dark alleys frantically searching — but searching for what? I knew I needed to be available for Tom and the kids as we put our home and lives back together. Still I seemed continually nervous and angry at everyone — including God. I asked myself, "What should I be doing?" I tried looking for an exciting job. I considered graduate school and various volunteer options. I prayed, but God seemed to be silent. So I asked my sister to pray for me because I needed help in knowing what direction I should take. Shortly after that I began writing — in secret. I'd wait until everyone left each morning, race through my morning duties, then hole up in my office and write.

About a week after I had begun to write, my sister telephoned. When I asked if she had any news for me from her prayers, she responded with regret, "No, sorry, Sally, I can't really say I have any sense of what you should be doing...." As we talked, news of a trip she'd made with Mom came up. "You know, Mom and I were talking about that letter you wrote, Sally. We both found it interesting and useful. You really ought to do some writing," she said. I had my confirmation!

I had asked another Christian to pray, and she confirmed my unlikely new direction in life. We need the Christian community. Asking another Christian to pray is a good way to confirm God's word or action in our lives.

Do I Seem to Be Controlling God?

When looking for authenticity in religious experience, notice whether you seem to be the one controlling your communication with God. If God tells you just what you expected or wanted to hear, that should be cause for suspicion. God is an active partner in the dialogue. Active partners are not absolutely predictable.

A friend described a time when God didn't tell her what she expected to hear. It doesn't even matter what God's message was. "I was so busy having a pity party that *I never heard God's message* the first few times he tried to contact me. Once I realized what I was doing, I began to let myself think and listen more carefully. I heard ideas I was totally unprepared for, was told to go places I had never wanted to go before. One day an idea 'just popped into my head,' surprising me. By this time I knew it was God calling again."

God wants to be part of our lives. Although there is no right or wrong way to develop a relationship with God, we must realize we cannot control the way God relates to us. God sets the direction of the relationship. We should simply look to God as he appears in Scripture or in our experience without setting up any suggested plan for God's action. Then just let happen what will happen.

One example of the problems created by attempts to control God occurred recently. At a dinner party a friend said, "Sally, I just can't buy into your claim that God speaks to people. I was talking to two pastors who had each prayerfully gone to God as they made a decision about the sale of a piece of property owned by a Christian school in Thailand. One insisted that God told him to sell; the other was emphatic that God told him not to sell. These are both prayerful Christians!" One or both of them apparently had an agenda for God. One or both of these prayerful men were trying to hold the controls of his relationship with God. It's easy to let our egos get in the way of our relationship with God.

When we want something very much, it is hard to let go and be honestly open as we stand before God in prayer. When we try to control the relationship, communication becomes impaired. Our relationship with God is fully interactive when we turn control over to him, allowing him to teach and guide us to closer intimacy.

How Can I Be Sure When God Speaks?

All these tests seem to indicate that I think I always know when God is speaking, but I am still frequently confused and uncertain. Even holy people who are very close to God don't always know immediately when God speaks. That makes a neophyte like me feel comforted in my confusion. At times I feel distant, like the lost lamb among the flock. I still wonder where God is. During these difficult times I sometimes pray solely because he promised to be with me. When he is distant I pray not from love or a sense of his presence but rather from a basic hunger for him. I just need him.

In summary, some ways that help me understand when God is speaking include (1) using everyday communication skills and (2) noticing feelings, thoughts, and changes. Additionally, I gain insights into the authenticity of messages by asking (3) Is it good? (4) Is it to my advantage? (5) Does it stand the test of time? (6) Does it promote a sense of urgency? (7) Do I feel enthusiastic about it? (8) Do I feel at peace? (9) Do I act as if I have control of

God? And finally I can (10) ask God for a sign and (11) ask another Christian to pray. In using these tests it is important not to set limitations on our development toward knowing God better. We cannot manipulate God; but we can, by recognizing God more readily, boost our confidence in him and move along in our spiritual journeys.

God isn't afraid to be tested or questioned. I believe God welcomes ways to make himself clear to us. God will help us along the way, but the responsibility to search is ours. We are the one with major limitations of sensitivity and skill in communication — not God.

CHAPTER 6

SURELY GOD
WOULDN'T CALL
SOMEONE LIKE ME?

I have told you about my spiritual development and discoveries, my fears and struggles. I have told you how I came to believe that God is alive, well and operating in the world and in my life today. In this chapter we'll review my spiritual journey and also look to the future. My story is not yet over and neither is yours. Our spiritual journeys build on our past spirituality. First, let's review my story in a few paragraphs.

After putting aside Church attendance and most other outward signs of Christianity, I began to go to church again "for the kids." I was comfortable with the assessment that some people need an emotional involvement in religion. I didn't think I needed it, but maybe our children would some day. It never occurred to me that adding Sunday Mass to my schedule would affect me in any significant way. Then at Mass one Sunday God touched me in a personal way. I was confused and scared. I had heard about people who claimed to have a personal relationship with God, but I saw this approach to God as merely a useful tool for the weak mind. Religion should be one small peg in the pegboard of my life, I thought.

Even after God offered me repeated experiences, I was wary of allowing an active God into my life. I abhorred some activities which I saw attributed to God — activities such as war or the collection of huge sums of money for personal mansions and a grand lifestyle. I saw people avoid responsibility by attributing their actions to "God's will," which seemed to become a quick and easy formula for them to feel good or get what they want. I didn't like imposing religion and morals on others or the know-it-all attitude I saw among professed Christians. Yes, my heels were firmly planted and the skid marks clearly creased the pavement in my attempt to resist God. I was afraid.

This fear urged me to search for an understanding of this new part of my life. As a result I learned to communicate with God. Up to this time I thought a few special folks were chosen to be touched by miracles as a reminder to the rest of us that there really is a God. Eventually, I came to understand prayer as two-way communication with God, even for me. I understood that prayer encompasses a variety of activities, and is, in fact, a way of life.

God used every means available to get me to understand. God knew I needed to be entertained, so he used music and speakers as an introduction to him. God knew I valued a quality marriage and family life, so he used marriage retreats to get me to focus on him. God knew I loved to read, so he used books to show me a variety of approaches to him. God knew I wouldn't accept a solely emotional experience, so he convinced me on an intellectual level as well.

God initiates communication with me as well as responds to me. God isn't vague, distant, or passive. I believe God when he tells me that he will do whatever I ask, as he does in John 14:

"And whatever you ask in my name, I will do, so that the Father may be glorified in the Son. If you ask anything of me in my name, I will do it."

(John 14:13-14)

Scripture indicates an active God, one involved in day-to-day events. I am comforted in the difficult times because he is concerned and interested in my physical, emotional, and spiritual well-being. I read the following passage from Luke in celebration of the good times and for reassurance in bad times because I believe he means it when he says:

"Therefore I tell you, do not worry about your life and what you will eat, or about your body and what you will wear. For life is more than food and the body more than clothing. Notice the ravens: they do not sow or reap; they have neither storehouse nor barn, yet God feeds them. How much more important are you than birds! Can any of you by worrying add a moment to your lifespan? If even the smallest things are beyond your control, why are you anxious about the rest? Notice how the flowers grow. They do not toil or spin. But I tell you, not even Solomon in all his splendor was dressed like one of them. If God so clothes the grass in the field that grows today and is thrown into the oven tomorrow, will he not much more provide for you, O you of little faith?"

(Luke 12:22-28)

As I began to believe that God indeed cared about me personally, I could accept God's love. This freed me to explore methods of communication with God. I needed confidence in God's love before I was willing to share myself with him just as I need confidence in a friend's love before I am willing to share myself with her. I have shared some of what I have learned about the ways

God speaks. These include God speaking through formal prayer, daily events, Scripture, forgiveness, using us as his instruments, suffering, nature, and music. These are only the beginning. It is God who teaches me to pray. God knows what I need to hear, what I will accept, and just how far to push me.

As I opened myself to allow God to respond, I became confused. I wanted to live with God as a guide, but I had trouble determining when it was God speaking and when it was Sally speaking. Almost without realizing it I began to develop ways to discern the difference. They include using everyday communication skills; noticing feelings, thoughts, and changes; asking for signs; asking another Christian to pray. I also ask these questions: Is it good? Is it to my advantage? Does it stand the test of time? Does it spark a sense of urgency? Do I feel enthusiastic about it? Do I feel at peace? Do I act as if I am controlling God?

These tests helped make me more comfortable with God's messages, but it is also necessary to take into account my own prejudices. In some areas I have been conditioned since childhood to think in a certain way. In these areas I must expect to have trouble clearly understanding God's plan for me. Money is a good example in my life. I am frugal. If I hear God suggesting that I do something which is expensive and isn't clearly a sensible use of money to my way of thinking, my first response will be, "Oh, gee, I must have heard him wrong!" So although these tests can be useful, I must also know myself and allow myself mistakes and uncertainty. These mistakes and uncertainty are not signs of abandonment by God but signs of my humanity. God is patient. He will walk through uncertainty with me. He will support me even in my mistakes, but I must be patient with myself.

This book encourages a familiarity with God from which I would have retreated only a few years ago. At that time I viewed God as one who had power and one who judged right and wrong; that God was not a friendly being. Through the Lord's Prayer I have now come to appreciate a new dimension of God. When Jesus taught the apostles to pray, he told them to praise God, ask for the things they need, and confess their sins. Maybe these aspects of prayer weren't so obvious in his own life and practices, or maybe they were more difficult for his followers. The most important lesson Jesus taught in the Lord's Prayer, I now believe, was familiarly with God.

In Jesus' time the name of God was spoken but once a year by the high priest inside the holiest part of the temple. Teaching the apostles to begin with "Abba" or "Father" was a powerful lesson. Actually, scholars tell us that "Abba" should be translated as "Daddy" in English rather than "Father," to give the true feeling of the word. This lesson in familiarity with God affects all the lessons Jesus taught his disciples while he was on earth. It was a dramatic change from the old way, a completely new side of the personality of God which Jesus wanted them, and us, to see. This familiarity with God, my Daddy, certainly affects the way I pray today. The distant Lord and God recedes; and the God who is familiar, affectionate, and loving appears.

I moved away from the Church structure I had been raised in. I was reintroduced to more than a Church structure; I was introduced to the experience of God. I moved through fear and curiosity and began to mesh the new ideas about God I was reading, hearing, and experiencing into a way of believing and living. I have new confidence in myself as one who is loved just as I am and not as I should be. I have new courage to step out and to take risks because I know that I have help always. Confidence and courage bring freedom. I am free to release old habits and ways of thinking which tied me down. I am free to release burdens and worries. I have freedom to make new choices for my life. I can be bold, even outrageous. Of course, with freedom comes the responsibility to seek God's will and live in awareness of and submission to it. Although this is hard at times, mostly it is an adventure and a challenge.

We Are Called in Big Ways and Small

We are called by God to play different roles at different times in our lives. We are called to be prophets for our generation. Prophets take daily events and put them into the context of God's will for us — now. It's not easy, though. Just as the prophet Samuel did not initially recognize the call of God, sometimes we don't either. Samuel's story is instructive.

One day Eli was asleep in his usual place. His eyes had lately grown so weak that he could not see. The lamp of God was not yet extinguished, and Samuel was sleeping in the temple of the LORD where the ark of God was. The LORD called to Samuel, who answered, "Here I am." He ran to Eli and said, "Here I am. You called me." "I did not call you," Eli said. "Go back to sleep." So he went back to sleep. Again the LORD called Samuel, who rose and went to Eli. "Here I am," he said. "You called me." But he answered, "I did not call you, my son. Go back to sleep."

At that time Samuel was not familiar with the LORD, because the LORD had not revealed anything to him as yet. The LORD called Samuel again, for the third time. Getting up and going to Eli, he said, "Here I am. You called me." Then Eli understood that the LORD was calling the youth. So he said to Samuel, "Go to sleep, and if you are called, reply, 'Speak, LORD, for your servant is listening.' " When Samuel went to sleep in his place, calling out as before, "Samuel, Samuel!" Samuel answered, "Speak, for your servant is listening."

(1 Samuel 3:2-10)

At first Samuel didn't realize that God was calling. He needed repeated taps on the shoulder and the advice of another believer. God had to say over and over again, "Hey, Samuel! Wake up! I have a plan for you." Still Samuel didn't recognize God calling. This happens to us today. It happened to me, especially in my early introduction to God.

I'd like to be able to say that when I recognize God's call, I always jump forward like Samuel and say, "Speak, your servant is listening." Unfortunately, it doesn't always happen that way. It's easy to think of reasons why God's ideas aren't sensible. Even Moses had this problem. He recognized it was God calling, but he made excuses. He insisted that he was nobody, couldn't speak well, and wouldn't be believed anyway.

> Moses said to God, "Who am I that I should go to Pharaoh and lead the Israelites out of Egypt?" He answered, "I will be with you...."
>
> (Exodus 3:11-12)

> "But," objected Moses, "suppose they will not believe me, nor listen to my plea? For they may say, 'The LORD did not appear to you.' "
>
> (Exodus 4:1)

> Moses...said to the LORD, "If you please, Lord, I have never been eloquent, neither in the past, nor recently, nor now that you have spoken to your servant; but I am slow of speech and tongue." The LORD said to him, "Who gives one man speech and makes another deaf and dumb? Or who gives sight to one and makes another blind? Is it not I, the LORD? Go, then! It is I who will assist you in speaking and will teach you what you are to say."
>
> (Exodus 4:10-12)

Notice how God reassures Moses. I will be with you, I will help you to speak, he told Moses. Typically we respond as Moses did. We think we aren't qualified, don't have enough time, or don't really think it is our job.

Moses didn't aspire to be a leader of his people. He tried to make excuses. God had to call Moses in a dramatic fashion. God confronted him with a burning bush. He turned his walking stick into a snake. He made his hand wither, then he healed it (see Exodus, chapter 3). Moses was stubborn, so God went to extraordinary lengths to convince him. For us, perhaps, the message will be more subtle. God will be only as dramatic as necessary to reach us.

We have modern-day prophets too. Martin Luther King, Jr., for example, pointed out wrongs in our society that we accepted as "just the way things are." He asked, "What can one person do?" Then with love and concern he demonstrated the power of the individual. Partly as a result of his effort we can now look with pride at legislation that thirty years ago we thought would be impossible to pass. Today our children can't believe that separate schools, drinking fountains, and restaurants for Blacks and Whites were once commonplace. My daughter asks, "Did you actually accept that? Did you do anything to protest it?"

Martin Luther King, Jr., didn't begin with his "I Have a Dream" speech. Mother Teresa didn't begin with a center for the dying. I don't know what specific actions began their calls. Possibly they wouldn't know either, but I think that surely God began with small requests.

Samuel, who was roused from sleep, didn't recognize the call to serve God. Moses recognized the call but had to be convinced by miracles of his abilities. Are housewives, military personnel, teachers, bankers, and clerks at the supermarket called to serve? Am I called to serve? When we, like Samuel and Moses, recognize God in our lives and accept our ability to serve, we will certainly be called to be prophets for our generation. Each one of us is called by God to affect her workplace and community, his home, school, or church in some small way. Responding to God's will is an integral part of the spiritual journey. When we recognize God in our lives, we also recognize our new responsibility to submit to the will of God.

My First Call Is to Pray

I have shared my spiritual journey with you beginning with my initial fear when I was touched by God, my exploration in communication with God, my eventual belief that God is eager to communicate with me, and finally my expectations for the future. Yes, I do anticipate that God will call me to action, and as I grow stronger my tasks will grow more difficult. My first call, though, will always be to develop my relationship with God. But developing a relationship with God isn't based on methods, techniques, and tricks. My development in prayer comes simply from a willingness to let God love me. With this willingness will come intimacy. It takes commitment and persistence on my part to keep still long enough to allow this intimacy to grow; but I will learn — I will learn from the Teacher himself.

ABOUT THE AUTHOR

Sally Greiner Roach received her bachelor's degree in education from the University of Oklahoma in 1969. She was a Peace Corps Volunteer in India and taught social studies in California and Bangladesh. In Kenya she worked for the United Nations Environment Program and later was the director for Lutheran World Relief's Volunteer Program for East Africa. She has traveled extensively in the United States, East Africa, Europe, Southeast Asia, the Middle East, India, Western Samoa, and Ecuador. Her travels brought her firsthand experiences and appreciation of varied cultures, lifestyles, and religions.

She was raised a Catholic in Oklahoma. Although during some of her adult years she was only a nominal Catholic, she was reintroduced to the Church in 1980. Since then she has been active in exploring the ways of God through liturgical celebrations, retreats, reading, and prayer. She currently lives in northern Virginia with her husband and three children and is a student at the Washington Theological Union.